GOING PRO

Developing a Professional Career in the Music Industry

by Kenny Kerner

ISBN 0-7935-9594-0

7777 W. Bluemound Rd. P.O. Box 13819 Milwaukee, WI 53213

Visit Hal Leonard Online at
www.halleonard.com

Do it.

Do it right.

Do it better.

Do it harder.

Do it all the time.

Acknowledgments and Special Thanks

To my immediate family—my mother and father, brother Barry, and sister Joyce. You guys are the best. I love you all very, very much.

To my son, Demian, for his love and for letting me be his dad.

To Danny—until we meet again.

To my industry peers: thirty years is a long time to keep a job, so I guess I must be good! Thanks to each and every one of you for your help, cooperation, support, advice, and guidance. This is the greatest industry in the world!

To Chip, Holly, Tommi, and Boi, for keeping the fires burning.

I would like to thank God for my health, happiness, and soundness of mind; for letting me do what I love doing each and every moment of my life; and for allowing me to simply be, as I am.

About This Book

Going Pro is divided into eleven separate chapters (and plenty of extras) dealing with some of the most important topics in the music industry. To really get the most out of this book, it behooves you to read it from cover to cover before entering into any power meetings with industry heavies.

Some of the information contained within the chapters might be considered "common sense" knowledge. But how often do we forget even the simplest of things when about to enter into a multi-million dollar deal? So when you begin a chapter, don't skip around looking for the sections that only concern you. Read each page of each chapter. It just could be that the information you have stored away is wrong!

Here's the lowdown on how the book is organized:

Ch. 1: Bands

This first chapter is a broad overview of what it takes to form a band and stay together. From how to audition members and choose a name to how to prepare for a photo shoot or rehearse—it's all in here.

Ch. 2-4: Your Pro Team

Personal managers, music attorneys, business managers, and booking agents. When you're ready to get serious about your career in music, these are the experts you'll want at your side—your "pro team." They work for you.

Ch. 5-7: The Industry

Record companies, A&R reps, and music publishers—these are the industry players you'll encounter in your journey. You'll have to work with all of them to have a successful career in music. Learn about 'em now.

Ch. 8-11: Tools of the Trade

From songwriting and demos to self-promotion and schmoozing, these are the tools and the skills you'll need to thrive in the music business.

Finally, the book concludes with my own story in the music business, entitled "Rewind: Looking Back," and an extended Q&A session that both recaps and amplifies much of the book's most important material.

Because you never know when you'll need certain industry information, you'll want to carry *Going Pro* with you at all times. It's small enough to carry in your attaché case and big enough to help you survive a career in the music business.

Good luck!

Table of Contents

x **Preface**
xiii **Introduction: The Real You**

Chapter 1: BANDS
1 Auditioning Members
5 Leading a Band
6 One Chief, Many Indians
7 Two Cases in Point: The Knack and Mozart
10 Naming Your Band
12 Photo Sessions
17 The Press Package
18 Demo Tapes
19 Rehearsing

Chapter 2: PERSONAL MANAGERS
24 Management Traits
25 Who Needs Management?
26 Self-Evaluation
27 Management Options
31 Finding a Manager
32 Creating a "Buzz"
34 How Managers Find New Talent
36 Attracting Clients
37 The Management Contract

Chapter 3: MUSIC ATTORNEYS
49 Start Shopping Now
51 Attorney Checklist
51 Considerations and Complications
52 Who Reps Who?

Chapter 4: BUSINESS MANAGERS & BOOKING AGENTS
53 Business Managers
54 Compensation
54 Booking Agents
55 How Agents Work

Chapter 5: RECORD COMPANIES
58 Inside a Record Company
62 Recording Contracts
64 Don't Do This!
65 Names and Numbers

Chapter 6: A&R
69 Makin' Records
70 Knowledge Is Good
71 Don't Call Us . . .
72 Decisions, Decisions
74 Kerner's Klass
75 Kenny's Kids
77 Cartoon Boyfriend
79 Why Your Tapes Get Trashed
80 The Three A&R Deals
81 Signing Ingredients
83 The Three A&R Games
85 How to Get It Done, Really

Chapter 7: PUBLISHING

87 Copyrights
89 Mechanical vs. Performance Royalties
90 How It Works
90 Start Your Own Publishing Company
92 Hang On to Your Songs
93 "Music Publishers" by John Braheny

Chapter 8: SONGWRITING

103 The Golden Rule
103 Hit Songs vs. Hit Records
104 Observations
105 Structural Pointers
106 Dummy Lyrics

Chapter 9: DEMOS & PRESS KITS

107 The Demo
109 Choosing Your Best Songs
109 Pre-Production and Recording
111 Reproducing Your Tapes
112 The Press Kit
113 Artist Photos
114 Cover Letters
115 Following Up

Chapter 10: SELF-PROMOTION

117 Promote Your Shows
121 Press Releases
123 More Homework
124 Deadlines and Publication Dates
124 Paid Advertisements
125 Merchandising
127 "Self-Awareness" by Dennis Anderson

Chapter 11: MEETING & GREETING
139 The "In Crowd"
142 What to Say
142 Telephone Talk
143 Looks Can Kill
143 Getting Ahead
145 "People Power" by Dan Kimpel

149 **Rewind: LOOKING BACK**
172 **Review: Q&A**
190 **Recommended Sources**
194 **About the Author**

Preface

If you're preparing for a nice, lucrative career in the music industry, prepare to be screwed and ripped-off. There are no exceptions. You will be rejected, humiliated, neglected, misused, abused, overworked, underpaid, lied-to, mentally tortured, and frustrated in an industry where "Anything goes" is the daily work credo. Are you still there?

There are no rules and no laws in the music industry; only players. So unless music is running through your veins like blood, my humble and sincere advice is for you to pursue a career in another industry. Unless you need music for survival—like the very air you breathe—my advice is to get the hell out now!

This is an industry that rewards ignorance and incompetence. An industry in which failure very often elevates you to the vice presidency. An industry in which you may sometimes "fail upward." If you really are planning a career in the music industry, please check your emotions at the door. We don't want you to become the latest industry statistic when you discover that it takes a lot more than talent to become a superstar.

Do you have a fragile ego? Are you unable to handle pressure? Do constant ups and downs drive you crazy? Are you sick and tired of people telling you what to do? Is disappointment likely to make you put a gun to your head and blow your brains out? If you answered "Yes" to any of these questions, slowly put this book down and go back to college.

For almost thirty years, and against the better judgment of my parents, I have made a living in the music industry—as a record producer, journalist, personal manager, publicist, songwriter, and magazine editor. I became relatively successful at an early age and watched as a handful of managers, agents, and advisors systematically stole most of my earnings.

I watched... as musicians living on cornflakes and a prayer were ripped-off by greedy publishers taking advantage of a band's poverty and lack of music industry savvy.

I witnessed... as ruthless record companies issued recording contracts to artists—contracts that you wouldn't give to your worst enemy.

I trembled in fear... as I learned about artists who signed away 30% of their gross income to a manager who did nothing to further their careers.

I shook my head in disbelief... when I heard about a band that had all of its equipment confiscated by a promoter because the band didn't pre-sell enough tickets for their show.

And I almost cried... when I discovered that a local A&R rep pretended to be interested in signing a band when in reality he kept them in a recording studio for almost a year (leading them to believe they were in a development deal) just so he could brush up on his producing skills.

I wrote this book because it's the quickest and easiest way of reaching the most people. This book can save you. What I have found in my dealings with musicians is that, after several years in the industry, they begin to think they know it all. And in attempting to set them straight, I must first begin the long, arduous task of deprogramming them of the false knowledge they've accumulated over the years. Once done, I can program them correctly. This book is the program.

I chose to call this *Going Pro* because the advice, explanations, and scenarios in this book are useful now and forever—whether you are a performer, songwriter, band member, or just plain undecided about what area of the industry to enter. This book is geared to help you develop a professional attitude and professional career in this business.

> *Going Pro* means being able to function as a professional in a professional situation, even though you may have limited experience in the music business. *Going Pro* means that you have the attitude, education, and confidence to achieve success in your career.

During my almost three decades in the music business, I've compiled lists of the most frequently asked questions and have dealt with each of them within the pages of this book. *Going Pro* won't necessarily get you a record deal, but it will save you time and money by telling you how to do the right things the first time around. In other words, this book will give you a logical, step-by-step approach for getting your entire career on a totally professional track so that you can accomplish your music business goals.

Why waste time and money sending the wrong kind of demo package to the wrong A&R person? Why start auditioning business managers when you're not earning any income? If you sign with a publishing company first, will you receive the same monetary advance from them as if you signed directly with a label? You're into your record company for a few hundred thousand dollars, and they want to begin recouping some of their money from your publishing royalties. Is that OK? *Going Pro* deals with all of these pertinent questions and hundreds more.

I make no claim whatsoever about guaranteeing you success in the music industry. However, *Going Pro* will give you all of the necessary tools needed to survive. How successful you become by using these tools in combination with your talents and your imagination is the determining factor in assessing your longevity in this business.

—Kenny Kerner

Introduction: The Real You

What keeps many of us from achieving success in the music business is that we really don't know who we are. That's right. We may *think* we do, but we don't. To be truly successful in any field of endeavor, you must first know what it is you can do and what it is you cannot do.

A professional baseball team has a battery of coaches to instruct each and every player. The coaches go over every conceivable flaw in a player's fielding and batting habits and make him aware of his strong points as well as his weaknesses. For only after he is made aware of his weaknesses can a player overcome them and aspire to greatness. The very same is true in the music business.

All too often, musicians take on more than they can handle. Many musicians find themselves singing in groups—when they can't even carry a tune in the shower! Others feel it necessary to play lead guitar when they have barely mastered the three-chord progression. Then there are those who are compelled to write all of their band's material when they are having considerable difficulty in writing the alphabet. But why does all of this happen? Why do we take on more than we are capable of?

The most obvious answers are ego and convenience. Because we want to believe that we can do it all, our ego allows us to believe that we can. Because we don't want to go through the hassles and inconveniences of finding another lead guitarist, we conveniently tell ourselves that we play guitar well enough to handle the leads. No fuss, no muss. The results are, of course, devastating.

Before you set out on that long and winding road to stardom, know yourself and your limitations. Know what it is that you do best, and get others to do what they do best. If the very structure and foundation of your band is weak, your career will eventually collapse.

Be true to yourself, to your capabilities, and to your art. Don't let anyone, for any reason, tell you what to play or how to play it. Write and perform only what you feel deep inside of your soul—regardless of whether or not it happens to be popular at the time.

Remember that this is the music business, and if you play your cards right, you should be able to earn a living in this industry for many years to come—whether or not you ever get a recording deal.

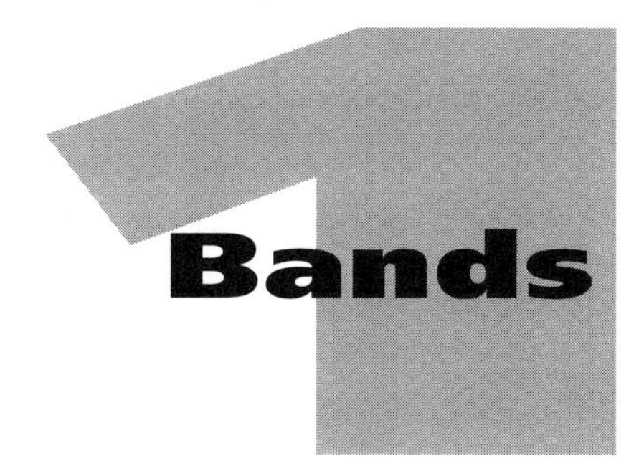

Bands

For the most part, bands don't work. They break up due to inner friction—usually within a year or two of being formed. And regardless of what former band members say, all bands break up for the very same reason: the players don't treat their band as if it were a business.

To most musicians, bands are cool. They help you get laid and make you feel macho. They're like hobbies; they make for some great male bonding and allow you to spend some time away from the girls. Being in a band sometimes makes you feel as if you're a rock star when you're really not!

But the truth is, if you don't set up your band like a business, you're wasting your time. Don't ever forget that you're in the music business. And the business part of it is every bit as important as the music part.

A band is the vehicle you choose to help get your music across to the people. It must be comprised of members who all share the same focus, the same vision, and who are all willing to make the same efforts and sacrifices toward succeeding. So, just how does one go about finding these people? Well, unless you're one of the lucky ones who grew up with a best buddy who happens to play guitar, you'll have to go through the rigors of auditioning band members.

Auditioning Members

The first and easiest way to look for new band mates is to place a free ad in a local magazine, fanzine, or newspaper. But even that can backfire if you don't say exactly what you mean. A short and simple ad that reads "Rock guitarist wanted for Valley band," tells you virtually nothing. If you run that ad, you're likely to spend hours on the phone explaining what it is that you're really looking for. A better ad reads like this: "Male rock guitarist, 17-25, with image, wanted to form new Valley band, into Van Halen." In less than twenty-five words, you've given every potential caller an exact indication of what you want in a new guitarist. By saying "into Van Halen," you've also answered the question of what kind of music you play. Rock, obviously! So, take your time, and write out your ad several times until every word is perfect. Remember, once it appears in a paper, it's too late to change anything.

Although running an ad in a local paper is a smart way to start, the most direct way to recruit new players is simply to steal them from existing bands. To do this, merely hang out at your favorite clubs, and check out the local talent while they are performing. You couldn't ask for a better audition! Also, the chances are pretty good that most of the people going into the clubs are either musicians themselves or know musicians. So, you win either way. You get to watch three or four bands play and check out those musicians, and you get to mingle with the crowd and get leads on other musicians.

If you see a great bass player performing his heart out to an empty club, chances are your band offer will be more enticing to him than what he already has! Remember—the grass is always greener.

Once you've found a couple of players that "feel" right, the next step is to question each of them to determine their focus, their sincerity, and their hunger to make it. Here are some things to consider when questioning a potential band member:

- Make certain that all of the members in your band are approximately the same age. Someone too young or too old will likely have different interests. An ideal situation would be to have everyone sharing the same band experiences in the same band at the same time.

- If potential band members have boyfriends or girlfriends, find out how serious they are. Tough as it may sound, someone who cares more about his or her sexual partner is not gonna last long in any band. Here's where the word FOCUS really comes into play. Keep in mind that Yoko Ono pretty much broke up the Beatles! If your boyfriend or girlfriend comes before your career, there's real trouble ahead. Enough said.
- Be certain to personally check out your musicians' equipment before telling them that they're in the band. A serious musician should always be prepared with his/her equipment and a spare. Be on the lookout for excuses like—"I always borrow my friend's amp for gigs." That excuse means the musician is ready to blame someone else for his or her failure to be prepared for a serious career. The rule is simple: Never lend, never borrow—save yourself a lot of sorrow.
- Each and every player in your band should have his own means of transportation. If a musician has to rely on a parent, friend, or other band mate for a ride to a rehearsal or a gig, there's gonna be trouble again. A self-sufficient musician should have his own amps, instruments, band outfits, and his own ride. These are his tools. If he is missing tools, he's unprepared and will eventually hurt the entire band.
- Find out how each musician lives. Does he or she work? Where do they get their money for food? Who pays the rent? This will give you insight into their desires to pay for rehearsals and general band dues. Nobody should get a free ride. Nobody should have to pick up the slack for a lazy band member. If band members have to work all day to afford a rehearsal studio, they will appreciate it more and won't waste a second when rehearsal time rolls around. After all, it's their money that is paying for the place. On the other hand, if the band leader or a manager is bankrolling the project, nobody will care

about being on time or about focusing in on the rehearsal. And why should they? After all, no money is coming out of their pockets! The tendency, of course, is to say that this will never happen to *your* band—but it always does.
- At an in-person audition, be prepared to play a tape of your material to potential new members. Don't give them the opportunity of telling you (six months down the road) that they didn't know this is what you wanted to play. Also, make it perfectly clear that you have no intention of becoming a different kind of band as the years progress.
- If you fancy yourself as the major songwriter in the band, lay it on the line from day one. Say that you'll be writing the bulk of the material but that you're always open to listening to other songs from within the band. Never close the doors to someone's potential to write or sing in your band. You never know when that might come in handy. And besides, if someone is being held back, chances are he isn't long for the band. Remember that the drummer in Kiss, Peter Criss, wrote that band's biggest hit to date.
- Tell everyone how you intend to run the band and what your game plan is. Will everyone have an equal say in band matters? Will you personally direct band activities? Do you intend to perform live? Record demo tapes? Seek professional management? Who are your contacts in the industry? What kind of timetable are you looking at? What kind of rehearsal schedule are you comfortable with? Don't keep secrets from the band members, and don't play favorites within the band.

I know what you're thinking. You feel that none of these things will ever happen to your band. But you're wrong. They happen to everyone. These helpful hints will eliminate hours of frustration and months of seeking replacement players. Besides, this is the proper way to conduct a business. And after all, your band *is* your business, right?

Leading a Band

Follow these tips for auditioning potential band members, and you're certain to come up with players who are likely to stay with the project for the long haul. But choosing the players is only the very beginning of having a real band. The first thing that every new band member will want is "equal rights" in making band business decisions and in career planning. Don't do it! Allowing all of the players to vote equally and make band decisions is truly the beginning of the end.

Right about now, you're probably thinking that I've lost my mind. That my twenty-five years in the music business have finally taken their toll. Put together a band, but don't let the guys in that band decide what shape their careers will take? Don't allow them equal say? Boy, you've really gone over the edge now, Kerner.

Not so! The problem with equal rights is that it is almost impossible to get any four or five band members to come to any one agreement on any subject—and if they do, what makes you think it'll be the right decision? Because all of the band members took part in the decision-making process does not make that group decision the right one!

Here's an experiment in terror that will prove my point: try to get all of your band mates to choose one group publicity photo. Sounds simple enough, right? Well, go on, try it. It can't be done. Here's what happens: each band member will look at a particular photo, and if he or she looks good in that photo, they'll approve it—never once checking to see what the other members of the band look like. Also, why should you assume that the other band members have an "eye" for art?

A band must be run by a benevolent dictator. One person upon whose shoulders fall the burden of moving this band forward. One person driving the train to the next stop. That person must have a strong, outgoing personality, a knack for networking and conducting business, a clear focus for what must be done, and great organizational skills. He or she must lead by example and not just run off at the mouth.

One Chief, Many Indians

The first job this dictator must undertake is to delegate certain band responsibilities to the remaining members. After all, a powerful chief cannot lead a tribe that has no Indians! By giving each band member limited responsibilities, you are giving them limited, controlled power and, at the same time, making each member feel important and in charge of a portion of the band's future. In addition to making everyone happy, this method also lightens your workload a bit. So, assign each member a specific band business job, and be very specific regarding what that job entails and how you'd like it done. Tell each player that at the beginning of every band rehearsal, the first half hour will be devoted to band business where each player will report on the week's progress. Believe me, if you treat your band like a business, there are endless jobs to take care of. Following is a partial listing of band business that needs to be taken care of on a regular basis—business that can easily be delegated to band members themselves:

- Scheduling band rehearsals
- Transporting band equipment to rehearsals
- Booking live shows
- Printing flyers to promote shows
- Distributing flyers
- Sending out press releases to local papers
- Coordinating the road crew
- Coordinating the band's live stage production
- Collecting names and addresses for mailing lists
- Coordinating equipment repairs

The list could go on and on, but you get the basic idea: *this is a business.* And as such, there is plenty for everyone to do if the band leader (that benevolent dictator) carefully doles out the responsibility to each of the other members. Keep in mind that no one job is more or less important than any other. Properly handing out flyers to promote your next live show is as important as booking the next round of rehearsals. The bottom line is responsibility and pulling together as a unit to move forward.

Two Cases in Point: The Knack and Mozart

At least two bands that I have known personally have been run by benevolent dictators: The Knack, back in the seventies, and Mozart, a local, Los Angeles-based band established in the early nineties.

During the blistering summer of 1979, amidst what radio called the "Disco Era," the airwaves were suddenly filled with a thundering of drums accompanied by heavy breathing and electric guitar riffs. Little did anyone know that this infectious rock ditty entitled "My Sharona" would put an end to disco and usher in a "new wave" of music in America. The band responsible for these four minutes of teen angst was a Los Angeles quartet called The Knack. Its leader, Doug Fieger, was one of the most famous dictators in rock history.

Fieger had the vision, the plan, and the ability to carry out his every wish. Though he co-wrote the band's material with guitarist Berton Averre, no band member was allowed to contribute to the decision-making process.

That privilege was reserved for Fieger alone. Did Fieger's almost omnipotent position bring about friction within the ranks of the band? Or, did the fact that he took charge of their careers contribute to the band's international success? Would The Knack have been as successful had the four band members been given equal rights within the band? Here's how former Knack leader Doug Fieger assessed the pros and cons of benevolent dictatorship:

> *"One of the most important things a band leader can do is to provide focus to the various musical and extra-musical elements a group has to deal with. Think of it as the point of an arrow.*

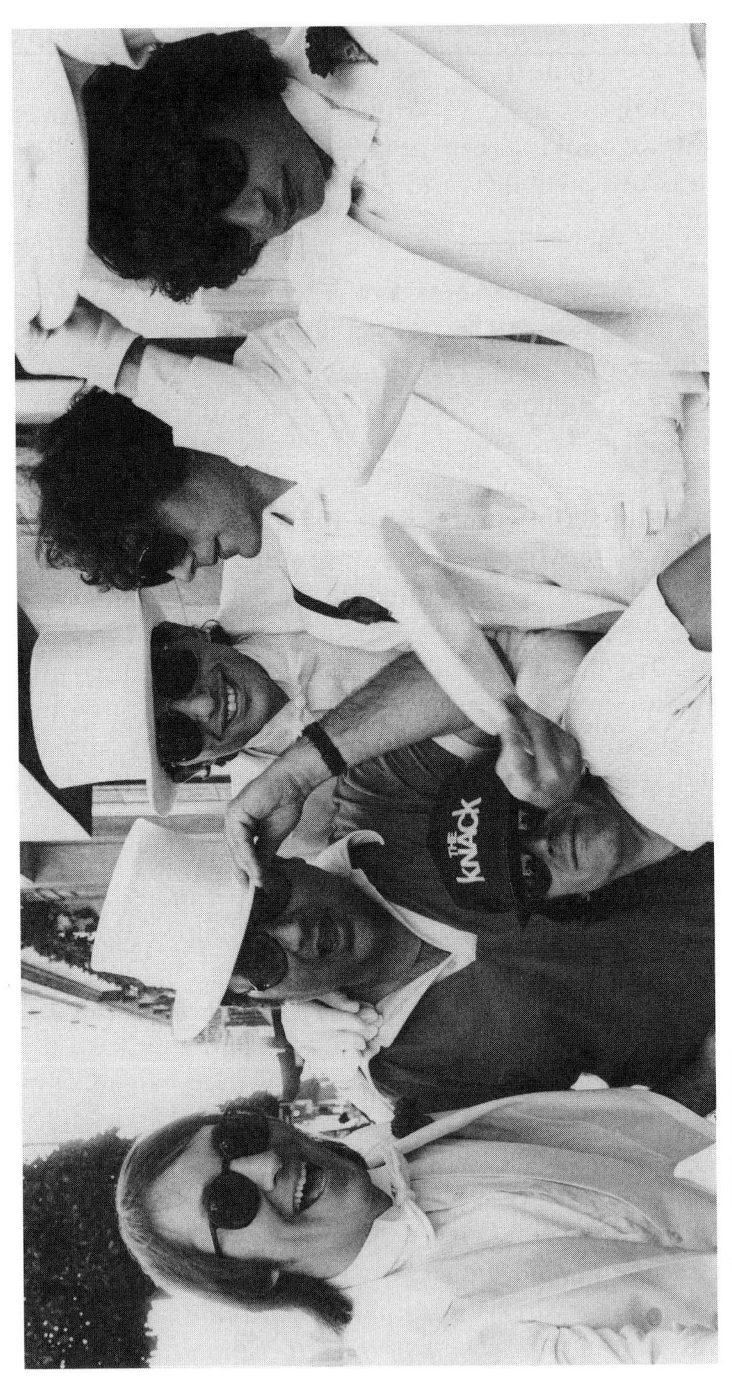

Kenny Gets THE KNACK
Once the Knack realized they'd made a mistake by shunning the national press during their meteoric rise to international fame, they hired me to be their press representative and make things right. Here we are, posing on Hollywood Boulevard for a rock magazine. From left to right, you're looking at Knack leader Doug Fieger, me (Kenny Kerner), band assistant Jeff Conroy (with the promotional hat), drummer Bruce Gary, bassist Prescott Niles, and guitarist Berton Averre.

The sharper the point (or focus), the more effective the penetration (or idea). In my experience, this is best accomplished by one, or at most two, strong leaders. Democracy dulls the point, and therefore the ideas are less effective. With regard to The Knack, I do think my focus had a lot to do with the fact that we were so successful. Later on in the band's career, when the other guys wanted to have more input, I think we became less focused, and we also became less successful."

In the spring of 1991, opera-rock band Mozart signed a megabucks recording deal with one of the hottest labels around—Charles Koppelman's SBK Records. The band was signed after performing only four sold-out local concerts and still had no less than seven other major labels bidding for their services.

With Mozart, everyone pulled his own weight. Adam, the lead singer, was in charge of the band's music; Ralph, the drummer, handled business affairs; James, the bassist, was in charge of press and public relations; and guitarist Peter watched over their truckload of equipment. Though not a total dictatorship, Adam and Ralph clearly ran the band—and not a single move was made without their approval. Adam explains how Mozart, as a band, took care of business:

"When a band first starts out, usually the one who starts the band runs the band. But I've come to realize that the one who is most able should be the one to run the band. In our case, it's our drummer, Ralph. If you determine for yourself that the need for the group's success is greater than your own personal ego, then you'll also come to the same conclusion. A band of five or six people must be headed by one or two band leaders.

With Mozart, although Ralph handles the business aspects, each band member has an important responsibility. The music, the press, and the responsibility for the entire stage show and equipment are handled by group members on a daily basis. So, for example, when Ralph wants to know what's happening with the local press, he'll ask James, who is in charge of press. This way, everyone is equally responsible for the band's success or failure even though there is really one band leader in charge of business."

The concept of "one band, one leader," is likely to spark jealousy and backstabbing in bands that are comprised of immature musicians with little or no focus. The Mozart approach of "one chief, many Indians," seems to work best for all concerned.

Naming Your Band

One of the very first things you'll want to do to help with group unification and bonding is to choose a name for your band. If possible, try to avoid naming a band after a single member—avoid the Henry Rollins Band or Alvin Lee & Company. Naturally, if the band leader is writing all of the material, putting the group together, and financing most of it, you might not have a choice in the matter.

Like any other field, some names are good, and some aren't. Avoid names that leave you with a negative feeling. For example, Small Change doesn't really say much for the band's aspirations, whereas They Might Be Giants leaves you with an overwhelmingly positive feeling of success. The last thing you want to do is choose a name that will allow music journalists to rip you to shreds without having listened to your music.

Always choose a name that is positive and reflective of the moods and music of the band. The Rolling Stones is a perfect example of describing the members' personal lives, their music, and their attitude. Mountain, led by the massive, three-hundred pound guitarist Leslie West, suited the group perfectly. And Mötley Crüe couldn't have bought a better name. Are you starting to get the idea?

Choosing a name that is controversial can also be good, but be careful not to choose a name that gives off harmful signals. Calling your band the Nowhere Men is just asking for trouble!

You can start the selection process by asking each band member to compile a list of names. Spend a couple of weeks putting these lists together and then, at a band meeting, with plenty of beer on hand, compare lists. See if any of the names makes sense for your particular band. Maybe combining two names will work in a strange way. If nothing comes of this meeting, don't force it. Remember, once you choose a name, you're stuck with it. Forever. From experience, I have found that band names usually are discovered spontaneously—when nobody is making an effort. Someone will say something, and all of a sudden it'll click: "Hey, that's a cool name for a band."

Here's something you should remember when choosing a name: When a band becomes famous and starts having hit records, their band name automatically becomes accepted—even cool. The Turtles, the Beau Brummels, Strawberry Alarm Clock, ABBA, the Beatles, even Hootie & The Blowfish are all examples of silly names of hit bands. The point is this: you've got to live with the name of your band. You've got to be proud to say it, to write it, and to see it. And that's all that really matters. If you start having success in the industry, people will automatically think you're cool, and if you fail, who will ever remember?

If you can combine a great name with a great logo—Kiss, Yes, Grateful Dead—then you've got the best of both worlds. A memorable logo helps immediately with band identification and also serves as a handy marketing/merchandising tool.

Once you come up with a name you all like, live with it for a while. Ask your friends and other musicians what they think about it. Write out the name several different ways to see what it looks like in print. See if you can come up with a unique tagline or marketing slogan using your new name—for example, "Does your mother know you've been keeping Bad Company?" Or this one from a former Los Angeles band: "The Stingers—Catch the buzz."

If you come up with a great name that lends itself to a logo design, the next logical step would be to find an artist who can design your logo **"on spec."** All this means is that an artist will provide his creative talents to you for the cost of his materials on the speculation that when you get money (by getting a record company advance or money from an investor, etc.) you'll repay him in cash or allow him to do your CD cover.

While most artists will gamble and do a logo on spec, be forewarned: Make sure you draw up an agreement stating exactly how much the artist will charge you to purchase and own the logo outright. You do not want to have to pay a fee to the artist every time you use your own logo! Naturally, you'll want to have this discussion before the artist spends his time and efforts on the work.

Without this agreement, you can count on the artist to sue you for thousands of dollars as soon as you come into any money at all. Keep reminding yourself that *this is a business!*

Photo Sessions

Now that your band has a name (and in some cases a logo), it's time to set up a professional photo session so that you'll have some promotional tools to pass around. Much like the artist who created your logo on spec, many photographers can also be talked into shooting your band for cost and a promise.

One very important thing to keep in mind is that *you* want to eventually own all of the photos from that session. You do not want to walk away with two black and white 8x10s while the photographer keeps the remainder of the session, selling them to you one photo at a time (or even worse, selling photos to magazines for money—photos that you, as a band, may not approve!). Again, this must be made part of your agreement up front. Don't be afraid to tackle hardcore business problems like discussing money or control. Your choice is to deal with them now or have them come back to bite you on the ass later. And they always do! Tie up all of your loose ends. Control everything you possibly can. It's good business.

Keep in mind that photo sessions are not free-for-alls. They are an important band activity and must be taken seriously by everyone. Here are some important tips to follow when preparing for your group photo session:

- Meet with your entire band, and tell them you are going to schedule a group photo session in the near future. Try to give everyone at least six weeks notice before the actual shoot. Ask them to begin thinking about what clothes and image they want to project. Go shopping together, and pick out clothes that are cost-effective and compatible with the band's image and attitude.
- Give everyone in the band a deadline for shopping and coming up with at least three different changes of clothes. Band members may have appropriate clothes at home, and not everything need be bought.
- Go over each member's choices, and be sure nobody is wearing the same outfit. Make certain that clothes fit properly and are not ripped or torn (unless that's your particular image). Have all clothes cleaned so that they look new and fresh and special. Set aside proper jewelry—earrings, bracelets, etc. Then, when everything is together, pack all of your photo-session clothes, jewelry, and shoes in a travel bag (one that carries suits so it doesn't fold and get wrinkled), and set it aside until the photo session day.
- Now that your clothes are together, it's time to get *yourself* together—personal grooming, I mean. If you're going to get your hair cut, keep in mind that you'll need at least an extra two weeks or more for some of it to look like it's grown back. Don't cut your hair on Monday, and wonder why it looks so short at your photo session on Wednesday!
- Don't lose your mind entirely. Here's a sample phone call certain to give any manager ulcers:

  [Telephone rings at manager's house, and manager answers.]

  "Hello."

  "Hello, Kenny? This is Gary. I'm at the hair salon, and Stacy here thinks my hair would look great with a purple tint. What do you think?"

> "Well, Gary, we have a photo session in one week. What if the purple tint looks awful? What if it doesn't exactly look purple?"
> "Well, I asked Stacy, and she said it would probably all wash out in time with little or no damage to my hair..."

Do you get the point? Don't do any experimenting just before a photo session. Be natural. Take what you already have, and make it better. After the photo session, when there's no pressure, you can color your hair, check it out, see what friends say, and live with it for a while without being stuck with it in photos for the next year!

- Knowing that you have a photo session in about six weeks, you must now go about the task of getting yourself in shape physically. The best way to do that is to take off your clothes and stand in front of a full-length mirror in your house. Are your thighs too fat? Do you have a beer belly? Big butt? If you do, you've got plenty of time to visit the local gym and work it off. Also, taking off your clothes gives you a chance to check your tan lines. You don't want to do any photos without a shirt if your tan line ends at the elbow and the rest of your arm is ghostly white! It may sound anal now, but if you discover these things after the session, it's too late.
- Check your complexion. Do you have pimples that are visible? Have you been attempting to grow a mustache that you might now want to shave off? If so, you've got plenty of time to work on yourself.
- Now that you're in shape, it's time to scout around and find a reliable person who can come to the photo session and apply make-up and do the band's hair. This person should be paid by the band since he or she will be working during the entire session. Usually, a band member will have a girlfriend who can handle these chores for about fifty to seventy-five bucks for the day.

Make sure they have all of the necessary make-up, powders, blushes, liners, hair dryers, hair sprays, etc. Be sure to give this person the exact address, phone number, day, date, and time of the photo session as well as an exact time of arrival. Tell him/her you will pay in cash and you want a receipt. Remember, this is a tax deduction!

- While all of this personal grooming is going on, schedule a meeting with the photographer to lock into a specific date for the session and to exchange creative ideas. It's a great idea to give the photographer a tape of your music and a photo of the band so he or she can get some kind of idea as to what you're all about.
- Tell the photographer how you want the band to look—hard, soft, serious, lighthearted, and fill him in on some of the individual quirks of the members. Sometimes, one of the members is terribly short, and the photographer will need to place that person in the back or on the side of the set and stand him on a box that is hidden. Knowing this in advance will help. Keep in mind that the photographer also has to prepare for the photo session!
- Never schedule a photo session for early in the morning. Always allow everyone to get a good night's sleep and show up rested.
- Try to do your session indoors at a photo studio as opposed to outdoors where the glare from the sun or an overcast, cloudy sky might present a problem.
- Remove all wristwatches, clocks, and calendars from the set. Nobody needs to know on what day and time you were photographed.
- With each clothing change, try to also change the color of the backdrop. This gives the impression of more than one photo session.

- Bring a cassette player and some tapes or CDs to the session, and turn up the volume. This will wake everyone up and keep them alert. Inspiration, baby.
- Be sure that nobody in the band is eating or chewing gum while photos are being taken. The camera doesn't lie. You don't want to discard good photos because gum was hanging out of the bass player's mouth.
- Have your make-up person constantly check everyone for running make-up, shiny noses, sweat, etc.
- Ask your photographer to shoot in both color and black & white. Getting your photos back as 35mm color slides gives you the option of going full color or converting a color slide to B&W.
- Take both group and individual photos at the same session. They'll come in handy.
- It's a good idea to bring some light refreshments to the session—some chips and dip, some beer and soft drinks. This is to keep group members from disappearing during the session. You'd be surprised what some musicians would do for a six-pack of beer.
- When the session concludes, be sure to pack all of your belongings. Chances are the photographer has another band in his studio tomorrow, and if they find your jewelry, it's gone forever.
- Thank the photographer for a job well done, and find out exactly when and where you can meet him to pick up the shots.
- Many photographers will turn the photos over to you only after they have rifled through the shots and taken out the ones they feel are inappropriate. Do not allow a photographer to do this. Tell him or her you would like all of the photos—regardless. You be the judge.

When you get around to finally choosing the group photo to be used for publicity purposes, be sure that everyone in the photo looks good. The photo should portray the attitude of the band. A stranger should be able to look at the photo and know what kind of music the band plays.

When printing up large quantities of these photos for distribution, be sure the band's name and/or logo appears on every print. The band's name should be the biggest word on the photo. You'll also want to list a contact name and number (phone and fax)—a manager, agent, publicist. And don't forget to print the photographer's name along the side of the photo in a small type size. He'll appreciate the free publicity, and if it brings him any additional business, he'll be more likely to do you another favor.

The Press Package

With the group photos taken care of, you now need only two more components to fill your professional press package: a band biography or fact sheet and, of course, a demo tape.

The band bio/fact sheet is a quick way of giving the press or fans insight into the band and its members. The differences between a bio and a fact sheet are simple: **bios** are usually two-to-three page stories about how the band formed, their influences, their goals. **Fact sheets** are individual pages—one for each band member—listing just the pertinent facts: name, instrument played, where born, personal influences, etc. Either is acceptable on a professional level, but, regardless of which route you choose, be certain that your bio or fact sheet is well-written, interesting to read, original, and that it contains plenty of information—useful information. It is not important to know that Johnny wanted to be a drummer since he was five years old. Now, if Johnny's been *playing* drums since he was five—well, that's another story entirely!

The most challenging job when writing a band bio is to make sure all of the facts are accurate. Check and double-check the spelling of each member's name. Do not assume that John is spelled J-O-H-N. It could be spelled J-O-N and still be correct! Always ask.

Don't make the bio too long. Nobody wants to read a book.

They want to check out a page or two and move on to the music. So be brief but interesting.

Demo Tapes

Most bands don't have a clue about how to make a proper demo tape. You don't need thousands of dollars and a professional record producer. Like photographers, many demo studios will give you studio time on spec if they believe in your music and think it's viable. So before you empty out your parents' bank accounts, do some investigating. Check out a few dozen studios. Keep in mind these are demo tapes, and you don't necessarily need a 48-track, state-of-the-art digital, fully automated studio!

The key to making an exciting demo tape is proper preparation. Know which are your three or four best songs. The key word here is "best"—not the songs that your friends like most, but your best songs—the ones that are well-written and perfectly arranged. The ones that most represent the musical direction of the band.

Be careful here. Many bands are talented and can write and play various styles of music. Only record the songs that represent the true style of the band. If you are a hard rock band, but at rehearsals you jam on a country tune to warm up, do not record that country tune regardless of how well you perform it! You will confuse everyone. Industry mavens need to have a clear vision of how to market your material, and if you play country and hard rock they won't know which way to turn.

Always rehearse the songs in a cheap rehearsal studio before going in to record. Better to spend $100 at a rehearsal studio than to waste a day in a recording studio arranging your songs. It's all in the preparation. If at all possible, invite your recording engineer/producer down to the rehearsals so he/she can get familiar with the songs. This also saves time in the studio.

At rehearsals, perform the three or four selected songs instrumentally—without any vocals. This is how you're likely to record them, so you might as well get used to doing it at rehearsal. Work out the solo sections note for note, and decide how the songs will end—fading them out or ending cold. Remember this: in the studio, you want to spend most of the time recording, not working out the arrangements.

Most bands are disappointed with the outcome of their demo tapes because they were unable to communicate with their engineer regarding the appropriate sound of their instruments. If you want your guitars to sound ripping and distorted like Green Day or Offspring, bring in one of their tapes and play it in the studio for the engineer. Very simply say, "I want my guitar to sound like this..." Then play the tape. Have the rest of the band do the same with their own instruments. This way, your engineer uses the records you brought in as a barometer for your sound, and everyone is happy.

Once your demos are recorded, mixed, and mastered, be certain to bring them to a reputable duplicating company. There's nothing more disappointing than making a great-sounding demo and having a cheap copy made. Be sure the song titles, band name, and contact name and number are all correct on every single tape copy. Ask the store rep for a proof before he runs off a few hundred copies that are incorrect.

Now that you have your professional demo tape, your band photo, and a bio/fact sheet, your press package is complete. All that's missing is a clean presentation folder (top of the line folders usually cost about $1.25 each), and you're ready for action!

Rehearsing

Take your completed press packages, and put them in a nice, clean place, because you won't be using them for a while. At this point in your career, if you are not careful, you could walk right into the biggest trap facing unsigned bands. I call it the "Let's-Get-a-Record-Deal" trap. For some bizarre reason, most bands feel that since they now have a press package, they have earned the right to get a recording contract. Bull. You have now earned the right to rehearse, play live gigs, and try to become one of the tightest, most popular bands in your area. The band that draws the largest crowds. The band with the best material. That's what you have earned the right to do. Succeed at this, and the record companies will be calling you.

Before you hit the live club circuit, you'll want to rehearse and get your act together. Rehearsals should be taken seriously. What you do at rehearsals is probably what you'll wind up doing on stage. With that in mind, here are some very important rehearsal tips to follow:

- Always check out a rehearsal studio in person before booking time.
- Find one close to your home so you don't waste time traveling.
- The rehearsal room you choose should be spacious and air-conditioned.
- Keep your rehearsal room neat and clutter-free. You'll be spending many hours there.
- If you plan on rehearsing for a month or more, work out a deal with the studio manager.
- Lock into a weekly schedule that works for everyone.
- Rehearsals should always be closed—no girlfriends or buddies.
- Don't over-rehearse. A three-hour session, two or three times a week is perfect.
- Work on everything at rehearsals—including choreography, between-song raps, sequencing the songs for a live show, backing vocals, etc.
- If you are scheduling a three- or four-hour rehearsal, always plan for a short 15-20 minute break to relax and go for a soda or burger. This eases the tension and makes the second half more productive.

When I work with bands at rehearsals, I always break down each session into four distinct parts:

The Warm-Up

After all of the band members arrive and finally set up their instruments, you want them to work up a sweat and get into the rehearsal mode. Trying to get serious immediately almost never happens. Therefore, I usually like my bands to begin by jamming. Just plain performing classic songs—fooling around doing favorites, oldies, whatever. This warms them up, gets them ready and in the mood, and is fun all at the same time. Fifteen to twenty minutes of warming up is all a band needs.

The Instrumentals

Too many bands never really get tight because each member only knows his own parts and pays little or no attention to what anyone else is playing. So if anything goes wrong, everyone is totally lost. I usually have my bands perform their entire live set instrumentally—with no vocals at all. This allows each band member to hear (sometimes for the first time) what everyone else is playing, it's easier to follow musical cues when you know the music, and should anything go drastically wrong with the PA system at a show, everyone will know the music and be able to complete the song like a pro. This kind of practice also helps you become very tight.

The Vocals

Needless to say, it's difficult to sing live. With the crowd in front of you and your adrenalin pumping, it's almost impossible to stay on key. Therefore, group vocal rehearsals should be mandatory. Simply turn down the amps and perform your normal set. With the volume down low, you'll be able to hear the vocals shooting out and pay close attention to every word. This helps you work on the harmonies as well. Vocal rehearsals can be limited to thirty minutes a rehearsal. Just run through the set, and whatever you don't get to you'll finish at the next rehearsal.

The Real Set

After a short break, have the band come back into the studio and perform their entire live set. Having already gone over it instrumentally and vocally, there should be some improvement. Work on arrangement changes, solos, etc. Use remaining time to go over new song ideas.

Remember not to go overboard when booking rehearsal time. Never book six or seven hours a day because you'll wind up wasting much of that time. It's called diminishing returns—the more you rehearse, the less you actually accomplish.

My advice is to never rehearse the day before a show, but if you absolutely must, keep it short and light-hearted—and under no circumstances should you begin to learn any new material for a show on the night before!

Also keep in mind that the rehearsal studio is your place of business. Apart from managers and road crew members, it should be free of friends and other distractions. When your girlfriend shows up at her job at the dental office every morning, does she take you with her? Similarly, she should not visit your place of business. Regardless of what you think, once a rehearsal room is filled with friends (and all it takes is five or six people), the band always seems compelled to perform rather than to rehearse. After all, nobody likes to make mistakes in front of their friends, right?

As a final reminder, keep all paid rehearsal receipts. As a business, your band will be allowed to deduct these expenses come tax time.

Personal Managers

To achieve success in any industry, it is necessary to surround yourself with a group of professionals who can advise you and guide you in the sometimes complex, always tricky decision-making processes. One of the first official things a band must do, therefore, is to assemble a team of professionals who will work with them toward a successful career. In the music industry, this means assembling your **pro team.** Traditionally, the pro team consists of: your personal manager, your attorney, your business manager, and your booking agent.

Of these four, the selection of a **personal manager** to represent your career in the music business is going to be one of the most important and most difficult decisions you will ever have to make. The personal manager is the focal point of all artist activity. He or she must serve as manager, advisor, agent, publicist, attorney, babysitter, banker, parent, psychologist, confidant, friend, and just about everything else.

When your guitarist is arrested in Little Rock, Arkansas, for having sex with a thirteen-year-old girl at four in the morning, you can be sure your personal manager's phone will ring.

When your bassist is pissed because your lead singer won't let him sing a single song on the album, your personal manager will be called.

When your drummer is just plain bored, guess who he wants to speak with? You're beginning to get the picture. Unlike most record company executives, personal managers must remain accessible to their artists twenty-four hours a day, seven days a week.

In short, in addition to business smarts, a personal manager has to have patience, understanding, a knowledge of psychology, and stamina. He or she must be level-headed—someone who can roll with the punches and not fold if things don't go his way. And above all else, a personal manager must have a vision for his artists. He must be able to envision the act as a total success and then formulate a plan of attack to bring the artist to that visionary level. Think of him as a long distance runner: The personal manager is the only member of your pro team who starts the race with you and finishes it with you.

Management Traits

Legally, your personal manager (often simply called your "manager") is responsible for guiding your career by providing **advice and counsel.** But there are dozens of other traits you should look for before making your final selection. For example, a manager should be honest, trustworthy, sincere, well-connected, powerful, accessible, a motivator, an organizer, objective, and a good negotiator. The aim, of course, is to choose a manager who possesses *most* of these traits!

Another important trait, and one that is almost always taken for granted, is the manager's ability to manage both the "person" and the "artist." A lead guitar player in a rock band is first and foremost a human being, with typical people problems—his girlfriend or boyfriend, his rent, his car payments, etc. Unless his mind is clear and his vision focused, he can never succeed as a rock star. A good manager will be able to deal with the "people problems" in addition to the career problems. They are not separate; they belong to the same person at the same time.

Something else often forgotten is that the artist chooses the manager. The manager is hired *by* the artist to perform *for* the artist—not the other way around. This is an incredibly important power point. The artist can and should tell the manager what to do. The manager will tell the artist how he plans on doing it and will, if he sees fit, disagree with the artist and present an alternate plan.

Most artists hire managers by counting the number of gold and platinum records hanging on the wall. Managers do this to intimidate artists. They lead the artist to believe that if they received all of these awards they certainly must be good managers. Truth be known, these awards are presented to the artists and given to managers and close friends as gifts and tokens of appreciation. The walls of my personal management office do not have a single one of my eighteen gold and platinum records. I want people to be impressed with me by meeting me in person and by checking out my reputation within the industry. Wall ornaments do not make me a good manager.

Who Needs Management?

Now that we've discussed some managerial traits, let's take a look at three very important questions: Who needs management, when does an artist need management, and what kind of management is needed?

Any artist serious about pursuing a professional career in the music industry will need professional management. Period. But to answer these questions, we must first take a look at what the artist himself is responsible for. On the local level, regardless of where you live, some of your responsibilities as an artist will include the following:

- Songwriting
- Rehearsing
- Maintaining a functioning band
- Promoting local shows
- Making demo tapes
- Booking local shows
- Getting local press
- Mailing out demo packages
- Making follow-up fan calls
- Inviting A&R reps to shows

- Calling attorneys for advice
- Networking within the industry

When your band activities become so cumbersome that you are having difficulty writing, rehearsing, and performing because of all the calls, paperwork, and follow-ups, chances are you might need a personal manager.

Self-Evaluation

Once you've made the determination that you need a manager, you must make one of the most difficult decisions yet—that of evaluating your own talents.

Much like your relationship with a criminal lawyer in court, you must be brutally honest with your manager. To do that, however, you must first be brutally honest about yourself *to* yourself. Here's a self-evaluation test that you and your band members can take. See how you do:

1. How serious am I about my career?
2. Do I want a full-time or part-time career?
3. Am I focused?
4. Am I in control?
5. Is my entire band focused and aligned?
6. How much talent is there?
7. Is there desire/hunger?
8. Is there belief? Self-determination?
9. Is everyone willing to make personal sacrifices?
10. What are our weaknesses/limitations?

Remember this: Not everyone wants to commit to a full-time career in the music business. Plenty of musicians are in it as a hobby or to get laid or to pretend they're rock stars. Some artists become weekend musicians or studio players or producers and engineers. Not everyone in your band right now is willing to make the ultimate sacrifices and commitments to really go for it. And that's what'll drag you down. You can't fake dedication and desire like you can an orgasm. You either have it or you don't. And if four of five players in your band do have it, ask yourself this—do I want to drive a car with only three good wheels? Certainly not!

Going over this self-evaluation check list will get you ready for your meetings with managers. It will put you closer in touch with yourself and your band. But more importantly, it will allow your future manager to give you help in the areas it is most needed. And that will make you stronger and more competitive as the race begins.

Management Options

Not every artist needs the same kind of personal management. The kind of management an artist needs depends upon what's going on with his or her career at the time. There are basically four kinds of management possibilities to choose from. An artist can: 1) manage himself, 2) ask a friend or relative to manage him, 3) obtain part-time management from a professional, or 4) seek out complete personal management. Let's discuss these options, one at a time, listing their good points and their drawbacks:

Managing Yourself

Simply put, this means that the artist will manage his career and/or his band's career.

Good Points

- No management commission to pay.
- Can make career decisions immediately.
- Manager has no other acts to deal with.
- You *always* get it your way! (This is good for your ego.)

Bad Points

- Management takes time away from being an artist.
- Management may isolate you from other band members.
- As a manager, you have little or no experience.
- Your ability to further your career is limited.

- You have no real industry connections.
- Labels don't usually deal directly with artists.

So when does managing your own career work? It works just fine when you're in a local band, making local band decisions like "What clubs should we play?" or "Which photo should we send out?" or "What songs should we perform live?" Most often, the leader of a particular band will assume the role of band manager.

Relative/Friend Management

This is when, for the sake of convenience, you allow a band member's relative or friend to act as manager of that band. This can be a time bomb waiting to explode. Never is the saying "Don't mix business and pleasure" more true than in this instance. Although this is one of the most common occurrences with new, unsigned bands, it is also the alternative that seems to cause the most problems as careers develop and the act becomes more and more professional. Nevertheless, here are the good points and bad points of this selection:

Good Points

- You can concentrate on being an artist full-time.
- You have someone doing the calls and the leg-work.
- You won't lose favor with your other band mates.
- Your management commissions are low or nonexistent.
- A relative or friend is totally committed.

Bad Points

- Will your band take a relative or friend seriously?
- Your relative/friend also has no industry connections.
- Relative/friend may take management job too seriously.
- If something professional happens, he may think he's a real manager!

Since most baby bands ("baby bands" is a term used to mean new, local, unsigned bands) will generally use a relative or friend to manage their careers at the onset, I suggest that they draw up an agreement at the beginning of the relationship.

- Explain to the rest of your band why you are temporarily appointing this person as a band representative.
- Do not refer to your relative/friend as "manager." Always try to call him the "band rep" or "contact person" so it's clear from day one.
- Be certain to tell your relative/friend that this position is only temporary and that, eventually, you will be hiring a professional personal manager.

Tell your relative/friend that he can share in income as the band earns it, and that, if he works out, you'll *try* to find him a position with the band when there is money later on.

The following traits are essential to a relative/friend manager. Look for them:

- Should be able to take direction and follow orders.
- Should be good with telephone work.
- Should have good follow-through habits.
- Should keep accurate notes and records.
- Should be willing to learn.
- Should make a good impression with others.
- Should look a little more "together" than band members.
- Should have the available time to do the job right.

Part-Time Management

Part-time management involves asking a professional manager or management company for help on a limited, part-time basis. In this instance, the artist will work out a prearranged agreement with a manager or company to discuss career matters for either a predetermined rate or for a small commission. Then, based on your arrangement, you can call, phone, or fax for advice.

Good Points

- You're dealing with a professional.
- You pay only when you use him.
- He's only involved in areas where you want him.
- You're not locked into him forever.

Bad Points

- His time is limited.
- If you're paying him by the clock, you must be brief and direct.
- Any complex situation will cost you lots of money.
- He's not committed to your career exclusively.

Complete Personal Management

This is when a personal manager or management company makes a commitment to be completely involved in the day-to-day direction of an artist's career.

Good Points

- You now have a full-time professional manager.
- He's only paid when you earn money! He's on commission.
- Because you signed a contract, you have time to develop a relationship.
- He's available to you 24 hours a day.

Bad Points

- You're signed to this manager for a few years.
- He's allowed to manage other acts in addition to you.
- The superstars he manages will always take priority over you.

When dealing directly with a large management company, you must beware of the "disappearing manager trick." Here's how it works. Usually, the new artist is signed and wined and dined by the head of the management conglomerate to show power and support. But when the ink on the contract dries, the artist discovers that his day-to-day career will, in fact, be handled by one of that company's fledgling managers—maybe someone fresh out of college with little or no experience at all. You're given every impression that the head of the company will be your manager, but then you get The Big Switch. Be careful of this, and *always ask* up front about who exactly will be in charge of your career. You don't want surprises in this area!

Finding a Manager

Before you actually spend time spinning your wheels looking for a personal manager, it is advisable to put together a checklist of things to think about:

Manager Checklist

1. Do I really need a manager now?
2. How well-connected is this manager?
3. What do I expect of him/her?
4. What does he expect of me?
5. What am I giving up?
6. Do I want a manager who is involved in the creative side of my career?
7. Did I check him out thoroughly?
8. Who else does he represent?
9. What's the "buzz" on this manager?
10. Will he meet with me in person?

This is a business where you make it happen. Do not sit back and wait to be discovered by a manager or record company. Go out and find them.

In New York, Los Angeles, and Nashville, it's a lot easier to separate the good managers from the bad because there are a lot more managers and more ways to check them out. But what if you live in Dayton, Ohio? Who do you turn to then?

Where to Look

- Pollstar magazine directory (special issue)
- Music Connection magazine's management directory
- Performance magazine directory (special issue)

- Ask other industry pros in your area.
- Ask local musicians in your area.
- Ask people managed by your potential manager.
- Ask local attorneys.
- Check the backs of popular CDs.

Tips to Remember

- Meet with your potential manager in his office.
- Go over your manager's checklist with him.
- Try to work on a ninety-day handshake agreement.
- *Never* sign anything you don't understand.
- A professional manager will almost never go up to a strange band and offer to sign them. He'll want to meet with them to be sure the band is real, too.

The two most important people you need in this industry—your manager and your A&R rep—both believe that any new artist worth his salt will find a way in their door. So don't be lazy. Get off your ass, and help make your own career a success. Remember, if you're not working on your career every single day, why should anyone else work on it?

Creating a "Buzz"

Like the A&R community, personal managers are trained to find new talent. And they look in the same places for the same clues. When discussing new talent, the first question you're likely to hear is, "What kind of a 'buzz' is there on this artist?" The key word here is **buzz.** Simply put, this translates to, "What's the word on the street for this act? What are people saying about this artist?"

So how does one create a buzz?

- Selling out local shows.
- Constant rave reviews in local papers.
- Demo tapes getting response on local radio.
- Local paper/magazine cover stories and features.
- Fans calling record stores and radio stations.

- Releasing an indie record and achieving sales.
- Having people in a manager's office talking about you.
- Creating enough excitement so the industry can't ignore you.

Local Los Angeles acts such as Dwight Yoakam, Mötley Crüe, Poison, The Knack, and The Offspring all caused such tremendous excitement that industry insiders were forced to deal with them. For the time being, let's assume that you're one of the lucky ones to have captured the attention (by whatever means) of a personal manager who has invited you to meet with him in his office or to call him directly on the phone. In either case, remember these tips:

- Be prepared.
- Have notes in front of you.
- Be brief and to the point.
- Do not waste time.
- Your object is to sound serious and professional.
- You don't get a second chance to make a first impression!

In the event you meet with your manager in person, you must be prepared to leave him your calling card—your professional press kit. The **press kit** is a package put together to familiarize others with you and your music. It usually contains a cassette with three or four of your best songs, a black & white 8x10 photo, a brief bio telling about yourself, lyrics to the enclosed songs, one or two recent press clips if available, and contact names and phone numbers so you can be reached.

But remember—even with a professional press presentation, the manager may still not be interested. If this is the case, don't take it personally. Always keep in mind that no two people hear music the same way. And just because one or two people aren't interested, that doesn't diminish your worth or your talents. It just means that one or two people didn't appreciate your music. So what? There's a whole world out there, and you can't let yourself be stopped by a handful of people who don't get it.

If someone "passes," however, be sure not to burn any bridges or leave a negative picture of yourself. This is a small industry, and you never know when a manager will resurface heading up a label's A&R department. It's happened before!

How Managers Find New Talent

Up to now, we've been looking at everything through the eyes of the artist. Let's take a brief look at the other side of things—how the manager becomes a manager and how he goes about finding new talent to sign.

Much like the artist, every manager starts his career as an unknown. And every manager must also evaluate himself to see if he/she is right for that grueling job.

- Am I cut out to be a personal manager?
- Can I deal with the stress and disappointment?
- Where do I go for help?
- How can I learn the business and make connections?
- What are my strengths and limitations?
- Where can I get valuable management experience?
- Where do I find acts to manage?

Here's a great, inexpensive way to develop your skills as a manager. Find an artist/band that attracts your interest. Go see them perform at a local club, and take notes about their songs, their stage show, their rapport with the audience, their outfits, their overall ability to entertain, their musicianship—you get the idea. Then, wait two or three months and go see them again, bringing your old notes with you. Ask yourself if the band has improved in any areas. Did they get better or worse? Are they more or less professional now than several months ago? Then, here's what you do:

1. Approach the band or call their hotline and ask them to send you a press package and a recent tape.
2. If their music impresses you, see another show, and try to meet the band afterward.

3. Find out if the band in question is already represented by a manager. If not, tell them you might be able to help them with their careers.
4. Try to set up a meeting at your home, office, or an inexpensive restaurant to discuss your possible involvement with the band.
5. Tell them what you feel about their live show and their tapes. Ask if they have a career plan. Be logical, and be prepared to back up everything you say with industry facts.
6. Attend band rehearsals and give helpful performance and song tips.
7. Know in advance what areas you can be helpful in. Can you also do their press? Their bookings? Their merchandising? How many ways can you help this band move forward?
8. With the band's help, draw up a list of career goals to accomplish during the coming six months. As you achieve each goal, cross it off the list, and make the band aware of this.
9. Always explain everything you do before you do it. If you and the band have a difference of opinion, tell them so, but remember that it is the band's career and you can't force them to do anything.
10. After six months, if all goes well, you should be in a good position to talk with the band about management. If you've done this with two or three bands, you will now have a small client roster as a new manager. Keep in mind that the Beatles, Elvis Presley, and Kiss (to name a few) all rose to international stardom with guidance from managers who had nothing more than common business sense, a burning desire to manage, and a vision for their artists.

Attracting Clients

As a new manager, attracting clients will be a difficult task. You're going to be caught in that managerial catch-22, which goes something like this: You can't really be a good manager because you have no real experience, but you can't really get experience unless someone lets you manage them! What to do? Well, after telling everyone you can within the industry that you are looking for new talent, your only recourse is to go out and try to sell a band on your talents, your connections, and your belief in their music. And here's where you're left alone to your own devices. You've got to be convincing to them. They have to believe, without a doubt, that you're good for their career—right now! (Keep in mind that any experiences at all within the industry—internships at management or record companies, for example—are always to your advantage.)

With good old persistence, and a little luck, you'll soon be the proud owner of a new, unsigned artist. But for you, the manager, things have only just begun. The artist-manager relationship is always a two-way street, and so the initial in-person meeting is also vitally important from the manager's perspective. Like the artist, a manager's concerns are many:

- Why did the artist come to me?
- Are his goals reasonable or outrageous?
- Can I help him achieve his career goals?
- Am I on the same artistic wavelength as this artist?
- Are my connections strong enough?
- Why do I want to manage this artist?
- Will this artist take management direction?
- Do I have the time to work with this artist full-time?
- How much *real* talent is there?
- Does the artist have a place to live and create?
- Does he/she have a problem with drugs or alcohol?
- Is his relationship with his boyfriend/girlfriend as important as his career?
- Do I detect any dissension within the band?

- Are there any existing contracts that are still valid?
- Is the artist heavily in debt to anyone?
- Is the artist himself willing to work toward his own success?

The next step is to solidify this relationship in writing.

The Management Contract

Most often, when first entering into a new relationship, both artist and management are reluctant to discuss money and contracts. Sometimes, an artist and a manager will just shake hands on their deal. Sometimes, they will avoid talking about it completely and just jump into the creative process.

Take it from me, regardless of how awkward it might seem, ask to see a copy of your manager's contract *before* he starts to work on your career. Believe me, it's the lesser of two evils! Otherwise, you're asking for real trouble. Check it out: You and your manager agree to work together, but no contract talks are initiated. Six months down the line, several record companies are extremely interested, and one or two have put solid offers on the table. Smelling money and success, your manager now presents you with his contract, but you find it totally unacceptable!!! Trying to negotiate with the manager holding a recording deal over your head puts you in a lose-lose situation! The time to negotiate is before anything happens. *Before* there is interest.

Here are some important contract features to know about:

Advise and Counsel

The two most famous words in every management contract are "advise" and "counsel." And basically, that is all a manager is responsible for to legally carry out his duties. Most of a manager's duties as listed contractually are in such terms as "consult with," "supervise," "represent," "confer with," "cooperate with" . . . —you get the idea. Simply put, the personal manager is the professional liaison between the artist and all of his functions within the music business.

To get a manager to include anything special in the contract—anything unusual that both of you worked out—you must include what is called a **rider** to the contract. A rider is basically an addendum to the contract; something tacked on to the contract—not initially a part of the contract but now binding. A rider may include certain career goals that need to be achieved by a certain time period, a chart of artist earnings that need to be met, or almost anything specific agreed upon by both parties but not part of a traditional management contract.

Power of Attorney

This clause authorizes the manager to act as an agent/attorney, enabling him to sign checks issued to the band and to deduct his commissions and deposit the remainder in the band accounts.

In most cases, with the artist in town and available, the manager will simply call the artist to the office to sign checks as they are received. Regardless of the situation, you should always get authorized receipts for all monies received and a complete monthly statement showing all incoming and outgoing funds. Even if you are not interested in these receipts, you can bet the IRS will be!

Initially, every artist always envisions his manager stealing a large royalty check, signing it, and heading for the airport before the artist gets back from a long, grueling tour. It's a very natural thought, but this is something that rarely happens. If, however, you are that paranoid, you and your manager can always work out a system whereby he pouches (e.g., by Federal Express) money to you overnight when you're on the road, and you pouch it back the next day from your new city. There's always a way of working out these details so that everyone is happy!

Employment Agency Disclaimer

All management contracts in the state of California (and in most other states as well) disclaim any duty to obtain employment for an artist. In other words, your personal manager is not a licensed agent and, therefore, is not responsible for getting you work. This "separation of agent and manager" clause was created because, in truth, a manager is perfectly capable of securing work for his artists, but if he does, what will agents do? They will have no jobs to perform to earn their 10%. To create a fair working relationship, it was decided to allow agents to book work and managers to manage.

Naturally, managers are not prohibited from confirming work with an agent or from discussing a specific job or its terms. As long as the agent initiates the act of procuring work, everything is fine, and he earned his commission. See, there's always a way around everything if you think hard enough!

What all this means, of course, is that now the poor artist must deduct up to 30% of his gross earnings—and he isn't done yet, as you'll see as we continue through this book.

Management Commissions

Another crucial area covered in all management contracts deals with how much personal managers are paid—a touchy subject to say the least. For the most part, today's personal managers receive a commission equal to 15%–20% of an artist's **gross earnings** in the music business. This means that your personal manager is paid *before* a single penny is deducted for anything.

The key word here is "earnings" because there are certain amounts of money an artist receives that do not qualify as earnings! Monies received for recording costs (to make a record), money received to pay a record producer, money given to an artist for tour support, monies (costs) recouped by suing someone who hasn't paid you, and money given to pay an opening act on your tour should *not* be commissioned by your manager. *It is not income.* It is merely money passing from you to another person.

The thing to remember is that all of this should be spelled out in your management contract rider. If you do not want your manager to take commissions in these areas, put it in writing!

There are other instances when a personal manager should not commission an artist's earnings. Assume you are a famous songwriter like, let's say, Desmond Child. Although you're making millions as a writer, you now decide that you also want to be a recording artist. So, you go out and hire a personal manager to get you a record deal so that you can record. Under these circumstances, your new manager is only entitled to commission the income you earn as a recording artist. He cannot take a piece of the monies you've been earning for years as a writer. Again, put it in writing so there are no mistakes or misunderstandings.

Actors Johnny Depp and Keanu Reeves are both in musical groups (P and Dogstar, respectively) with recording contracts. Their music business personal managers (if they've hired ones) cannot get royalties from the films made by Depp and Reeves.

Compensation After the Term

This is probably the most controversial part of negotiating any management contract. Every personal manager feels that he/she is entitled to receive royalties from artists forever. But is this really fair to the artist? Is it fair to be paying your personal manager 20% of your royalties long after your contract with him has expired, and he is no longer working for you?

On the other hand, if your manager took you from an unknown local street artist to international superstardom, is he not also entitled to a piece of those commissions forever? The answer, naturally, is a compromise—a sensitive issue for most managers.

Before you sign a management contract, it is important to limit the amount of monies and the length of time for which your manager is to be paid after he is no longer providing services to you. For just such a situation, there exists what we in the industry call "the sunset clause."

The object of the **sunset clause** is to outline the limitations of payments to personal managers after your deal with them is over. During the term of your contract, your manager is entitled to his full commissions. But what happens if he concludes a record deal for you just six months before your contract with him expires, and your album isn't scheduled for release until a year from that expiration date? When royalties really start to roll in, about 1½–2 years after a successful album, you will still be paying your old manager. Not to mention what you're paying a new personal manager if you've hired one. It is conceivable that an artist can pay away some 40% of his royalties to managers if he is not careful!

Here's just one example of how you, as an artist, can limit the amount of commissions your manager receives after the termination of his contract. Let's assume you've signed a management contract for a term of five years:

1. Your manager should receive his entire commission on all deals negotiated and on all records released during those five years.
2. You might want to offer to pay him full commission on any records released during the first three years *after* termination.
3. After that three-year period, manager commissions are cut in half for an additional two years.
4. Five years after the management contract has expired, your manager is receiving no commission at all from you as an artist.

This basically gives the manager five years of income for doing no current work on your behalf. Again, though, this must be dealt with when first negotiating points for your initial contract. Once you've signed, it's too late.

Also remember that this sunset clause must be discussed and negotiated together with your potential manager. Merely handing him an ultimatum won't do the trick. Keep in mind that negotiating is itself an art. A good negotiator always comes to the table knowing what he will be ready to give up and what he will not. You can do the same. Be prepared, but be fair.

The Cure Provision

Designed to stop artists from terminating their management contracts simply because they have a problem with their manager, this provision allows the artist to put his grievances in writing and give the manager a predetermined amount of time to "cure" the problem. In reality, it's like a "time out" for both sides to focus on a problem that seems to have been neglected.

Although each and every paragraph of a management contract is vital, these are perhaps the most controversial of all. Remember to take your final draft to a music business attorney and have him go over it with you. If you spend some time seeking one out, you'll be able to find a decent, knowledgeable attorney to review the entire contract for just a few hundred bucks.

I always make it a practice of working with potential clients for a period of at least six months before even mentioning the word "contract." After all, I want to be certain that the act is right for me, as well.

In reviewing your management contract, you will notice that there are usually no provisions for securing a recording, publishing, or merchandising contract. There's a good reason for this. No manager, regardless of how influential or creative, knows whether or not his band will be signed. To make such a promise in writing is foolish. Any manager who writes into a contract that he must secure a record deal for his band within ninety days is looking for trouble.

Managers are also responsible for the business end of an artist's career—like setting up a group bank account, making sure the band has health, dental, and equipment insurance, seeing to it that they are affiliated with a performing rights organization (ASCAP, BMI, SESAC), and in general, helping them to earn an income.

As an artist, you are looking forward to a relatively long and prosperous career—though nobody can even venture a guess as to how long or how prosperous. Therefore, it is important to come up with a plan for "the afterlife," as I call it—the time when your record sales are dwindling and there's not much interest in buying a ticket to see you perform. Don't laugh—this happens to just about every artist at one point or other. It happened to Kiss twice, but they were able to rejuvenate their career by first taking off their makeup and then, years later, by putting it back on.

So here's the message: Don't shy away from doing a well-paying product endorsement commercial if it adds additional income and years to your career. Don't scoff at the possibilities of selling color posters if it puts money in your pocket. How about writing a book about your career? Ever think about doing a movie? The point is that there are endless roads to travel, and all it takes is an imagination and a willingness to go where you've never been before. Happy trails!

Following is a sample of a current personal management contract that was prepared, to my specifications, by a top Los Angeles-based music attorney.

MANAGEMENT CONTRACT

Kerner Entertainment
6671 Sunset Blvd. #1505
Hollywood, CA. 90028

Jan. 1st, 2007

This management agreement is entered into as of this first day of January, 2007, by and between Kerner Entertainment, a Hollywood-based entertainment company, hereafter known as "Manager," and Mark James pka Mark Doe, William Erskine pka Hal Doe, Frank Worth pka Bob Doe, and Charles Batdorff pka Dave Doe, professionally known as The John Doe Band, hereafter known as "Artist."

Artist has carefully considered the advisability of obtaining the assistance and guidance of Kerner Entertainment ("Manager") in furthering artist's artistic, theatrical, literary, and musical career. Artist has determined that manager's services would be of great value because of manager's extensive knowledge and manager's reputation in the entertainment, amusement, and music industries. Therefore, artist wishes manager to act as artist's exclusive and sole Personal Manager for the term of this agreement, subject to the following conditions:

1. Artist hereby engages manager as artist's exclusive Personal Manager throughout the Universe for the term of this agreement, and manager hereby accepts such engagement. Manager shall be free to perform similar services for others and to engage in other business activities. Artist shall not, during the term of this agreement, engage any other person, firm, or corporation to render any services of the kind required hereunder.

2. Manager agrees, during the term of this agreement, to perform at artist's request, the following services for artist: To represent and to act as artist's advisor in all business negotiations and matters of policy relating to artist's career; to supervise artist's engagements; to advise and counsel artist in the selection of artist's material and in all matters relating to publicity, recording, advertising, and artist's live performances. Nothing contained herein shall require manager to perform or do any services which would be unlawful or contrary to manager's good faith judgment.

3. Manager is authorized and empowered by artist and on artist's behalf to approve and permit any and all publicity; approve and permit the use of artist's name, photograph, likeness, and voice, for the purposes of

advertising and promotion of any and all products on artist's behalf; to collect and receive funds as well as to endorse artist's name upon and to cash any and all checks made payable to artist for artist's services, and to retain therefrom, any and all sums owing to manager. Upon such time as artist hires a certified public accountant to handle artist's income, "manager's" rights to cash checks and endorse artist's name shall be with written permission of artist only.

4. Manager is not required to make any loans or advances to artist, but in the event manager does, artist hereby agrees to repay such loans and advances promptly. Artist acknowledges that manager has thus far advanced to artist the sum of: $ ___________

5. As compensation for services rendered by manager, artist agrees to pay to manager a sum equal to 20% (TWENTY PERCENT) of any and all gross earnings which artist may receive as a result of artist's activities in and throughout the entertainment, music, amusement, and recording industries. Without in any way limiting the foregoing, the matters upon which manager's compensation shall be computed shall include any and all of artist's activities in connection with the following: music performance, music merchandising, personal appearances, public appearances, records and recordings, videos, CDs, CD ROM, motion pictures, television, radio, literary, theatrical, publications, speaking engagements, and any and all other forms of musical communication whether now discovered or not (herein Entertainment Industry).

6. Artist likewise agrees to pay manager a similar sum of 20% (TWENTY PERCENT) of all gross earnings following the expiration of this contract with respect to any and all engagements, contracts, and agreements entered into or negotiated during the term of this contract and any and all extensions, renewals, and/or substitutions thereof and upon any resumption of such engagements, contracts, and agreements which may have discontinued during the duration of this contract and resumed after the termination of this contract.

7. The term "gross earnings" shall include all gross monies or other considerations received by artist, or which may be due or payable to artist, without deduction or exclusion of any sort, as a result of artist's activities in the entertainment and music industry prior to or during the term hereof, such as, without limitation, salaries, earnings, fees, royalties, bonuses, percentages of the total amount paid for a package television or radio program (live or recorded), motion picture or other entertainment packages, earned or received directly or indirectly by artist or by artist's heirs, administrators, or by any person, firm, or corporation on artist's behalf. Notwithstanding the foregoing, gross earnings shall not include recording costs, producer costs, video production costs, any collection costs incurred to recover monies owed and/or due, independent promotion

costs and tour support other than any such amounts as are paid or payable to artist other than as a reimbursement of expenses actually paid by artist.

8. The term of this agreement (herein Term), shall be for a period of 7 years (SEVEN YEARS) commencing on the date hereof. However, once a recording contract is negotiated on behalf of artist, the term of this management contract will automatically be extended to run concurrent with the full term of the recording contract.

9. Artist shall select a certified public accountant who shall be engaged at artist's sole expense. The accountant shall have the right to collect and receive, on artist's behalf, all of artist's gross earnings and deposit such gross earnings in bank accounts in artist's name. Artist shall notify and direct any and all gross earnings directly to the accountant. ARTIST SHALL NOTIFY AND IRREVOCABLY DIRECT THE ACCOUNTANT TO PAY MANAGER THE COMMISSIONS AND ANY AND ALL REIMBURSEMENTS OR REPAYMENTS OF EXPENSES FROM THE GROSS EARNINGS RECEIVED FOR EACH MONTHLY PERIOD WITHIN TEN (10) BUSINESS DAYS FOLLOWING THE LAST DAY OF EACH SUCH MONTHLY PERIOD, TOGETHER WITH A WRITTEN ACCOUNTING STATEMENT AND COPIES OF ALL STATEMENTS, CHECKS, NOTES, BANK DRAFTS, PROMISSORY NOTES, AND CASH RECEIVED BY THE ACCOUNTANT ON ARTIST'S BEHALF DURING SUCH MONTHLY PERIOD.

10. In the event that the accountant or any replacement thereof, is to be terminated, artist(s) shall agree upon a replacement. No accountant shall be terminated without approval of artist and approval by artist regarding the replacement accountant. Notwithstanding the foregoing, at such times as this agreement shall terminate or expire, artist shall have the right to engage any accountant on artist's behalf as artist determines in his sole discretion, provided that the last two sentences of Paragraph 9 remain fully applicable, and provided further, that, in the event artist has not engaged an accountant at any time after the term hereof, artist shall notify and irrevocably direct any and all third parties to pay manager the applicable commissions and reimbursements directly to manager.

11. In the event that either party receives any gross earnings to which the other party is entitled hereunder, such party shall immediately remit the applicable sums to the other party.

12. Each party agrees that the other party and its representatives may inspect, copy, and audit the relevant books and records of the other party upon at least thirty (30) days prior written notice no more than once each twelve-month period.

13. In addition to the sums required to be paid to manager, artist shall reimburse manager for any and all expenditures incurred by manager on

artist's behalf or in connection with artist's career in the performance of manager's services which are substantiated by receipts or paid bills. However, no more than $1,000.00 (ONE THOUSAND DOLLARS) shall be expended by manager during any one-week period for any one engagement without artist's prior approval.

14. Manager has advised artist that manager is not licensed as a talent agent/agency under the Labor Code of the State of California, or as an employment agent/agency or otherwise, under the Business and Professional Code of the State of California, or as a theatrical employment agent/agency under the laws of any state. Artist understands that manager has not offered, attempted, or promised to obtain employment or engagements for artist, and that manager is not licensed, permitted, obligated, authorized, or expected to do so. Manager will consult with and advise artist with respect to the selection, hiring, and firing of theatrical agents, employment agencies, talent agents, and booking agents (hereafter called "Talent Agents"), but that manager is not authorized to actually select, hire, fire, or direct any such talent agent in the performance of the duties of such talent agents.

15. Neither artist nor manager shall have the right to assign this agreement to a third party without the prior written consent of the other, which consent shall not be unreasonably withheld, provided that manager may assign this agreement to any person, firm, or corporation with which manager is affiliated or employed or into which manager shall merge.

16. Artist warrants that artist is free to enter into this agreement and to perform under its terms and conditions. Artist has had the opportunity to allow an attorney or another party of artist's choosing review this contract, and artist warrants that artist was not forced or persuaded into signing it.

17. No failure to perform any obligation hereunder by manager shall be deemed material or shall give artist the right to terminate this agreement or sue for or recover any damages against manager unless and until manager receives a written notice from artist detailing the default and manager has not commenced to cure the same within 45 (Forty-Five) business days after receipt of such notice, and effected a cure thereof within a reasonable period thereafter.

18. In the event of litigation arising from or out of this agreement or the relationship of the parties created hereby, the prevailing party shall be entitled to recover any and all reasonable attorney fees and other costs incurred in connection therewith. Artist also agrees to indemnify management and all management employees and representatives, from any and all legal action and/or law suits arising out of artist's live performances, lyrical content, press statements, or the performance of artist's duties as an artist in the entertainment industry.

19. Each artist represents, warrants, and agrees that each artist is over the age of eighteen, free to enter into this agreement that each artist has heretofore made, and that each artist will not hereafter enter into or accept any engagement, commitment, or agreement with any person, firm, or corporation, which will, can, or may interfere with the full and faithful performance by each artist of the convents, terms, and conditions of this agreement to be performed by each artist or interfere with manager's rights hereunder.

20. If the foregoing correctly states the terms and conditions of this manager and artist understanding, manager and each artist will indicate so by signing in the appropriate spaces below.

AGREED & ACCEPTED:

By: ______________________
For Kerner Entertainment

____
Mark James pka Mark Doe

____
William Erskine pka Hal Doe

____
Frank Worth pka Bob Doe

____
Charles Batdorff pka Dave Doe

070195

Music Attorneys

A good, honest, knowledgeable **music attorney** is an invaluable asset to an artist, and an important part of your pro team. Music attorneys serve many functions, the least of which is shopping tapes to the record companies. And because nowadays the top attorneys in the business (you know, the ones who charge $450 *per hour*) will work for a fee of 5% of the artist's gross income—why, anyone can afford them! Hold on a minute—I'm not being sarcastic.

Start Shopping Now

Just recently, one of the band's I manage decided it wanted to release its own indie record and sell it at shows. To do this, and to get the necessary UPC code, seller's permit, and resale number, the band needed partnership papers and hours of time to fill out applications for the State Board of Equalization, etc. This would have cost them thousands of dollars.

They also decided to have someone shop their record in foreign territories. This person wanted a contract to do so—granted, a simple one, but a contract nonetheless. More attorney time and charges. Fortunately, the band signed on with a top Los Angeles-based music attorney who is working for a percentage of their income. After reviewing their press package and listening to their tape, the attorney decided that this was a relatively safe gamble—that sooner or later, this band would be signed and would be making money.

By doing this now, when the band is unsigned, both the artist and the attorney have time to nurture a relationship. When presented with a recording contract, the attorney is already in place. The advance money the band receives will be commissioned by the attorney, but the process will not be held up because the band is poor.

The music business is abuzz with tasteless attorney jokes. Many attorneys deserve to be ridiculed, but the many honest ones (OK, OK, the handful of honest ones) deserve lots of credit for helping artists stay out of contract troubles.

Finding an attorney who is willing to work with an unsigned artist will take some doing. Like doctors, you need to meet with them in person and come away with a good feeling. But before you waste your time, consider that 95% of the music business attorneys today do not shop tapes to record companies. They consider it a waste of time—not to mention an exercise in futility!

Now just you wait a second, Kerner. Are you trying to tell me that managers won't work with unsigned talent because there's only potential and no actual money, and now attorneys won't shop tapes because it's a waste of time? How are we going to get signed?

Slow down just a second, buddy. There are many attorneys (the less expensive ones) who specialize in tape shopping, but these guys usually require a **retainer** (a month's fee in advance). Also, you must be certain to meet with them and find out how they go about this business of shopping. Since they do it for many other bands, you want to be clear about not having your package thrown into a giant envelope with a dozen other acts. You want your package and tape shopped under separate cover (meaning, by itself).

Each year, Music Connection magazine publishes a comprehensive and updated listing of music attorneys along with their addresses, telephone numbers, and other pertinent information. Buy this issue. Some of the most important attorneys in the biz are listed in that directory.

Attorney Checklist

Here's another one of my famous checklists to help you in the selection of a music business attorney:

- Who does your potential attorney represent?
- Is he/she aware of the contemporary music scene?
- Are his/her clients old, classic rock artists?
- Does your potential attorney hang out and go club-hopping or stay home alone at night?
- Have others heard of your attorney?
- What has he done in the industry?
- What are his strongest points? Contracts? Making deals? Litigation?
- How accessible is he?
- What are his hourly rates?
- Will he give you a client list?
- Will he work for a percentage of the band's income?
- What won't he do for you?
- How privy is he to "industry insider" information?
- How well-connected is he? A&R? Publishers? Managers?
- Do you feel comfortable when speaking with him in person?
- Most importantly: what's your gut feeling about him?

In the state of California, the law dictates that if you are working with an attorney and his fee will exceed $1,000 for a particular project, he must provide you with a written document itemizing and explaining his fee structure. If he's working on a percentage, this does not apply.

Considerations and Complications

Many artists underscore the power of the "heavy hitter" attorneys, but consider this: only the attorney and the record label know for sure when an artist's deals will expire. A band whose recording deal with Atlantic, for example, will expire in six months, might already be on the horn to Warner Brothers or Columbia, trying to light a new fire—in the strictest of confidences, of course. Here's where a nasty little thing called **collusion** comes into play.

If the artist's attorney talks Columbia into stealing the band from Atlantic without Atlantic having the opportunity to resign the act—and all of this is done in secrecy while the band is still on Atlantic—the attorney can be sued for "collusion." If this is too complicated to follow, don't worry. It almost never happens. I mean, bands are stolen away all the time; we just never find out about it!

Another complication with attorneys is the **conflict of interest** scenario. If an attorney represents an entire band, he should not also represent an individual within that band. In other words, if attorney John Doe represents the Rolling Stones for the purposes of their recording contracts, he should not also represent Mick Jagger's solo recording career—whether on the same label or not. There are bound to be conflicts making the attorney choose sides.

If this situation already exists, the attorney must notify the entire band and make them aware of it. It's then up to the band to decide if they want to continue with this attorney or find a new one.

Who Reps Who?

Keep in mind that we all want an attorney with a lot of power—one who merely picks up the phone and intimidates a label president into signing his acts. Keep dreaming.

However, the more powerful an attorney—the more clout he has—the more likely he is to do things his way. So be forewarned. As is the case with the rest of your pro team—your manager, your agent, and your business manager—your music attorney also works for you! Don't be afraid of power. Use it for your best efforts but be sure that *you* benefit from it and not just the attorney.

4 Business Managers & Booking Agents

We've looked at personal management and attorneys in detail, so now let's take a quick look at the remaining members of your pro team: your business manager and your booking agent.

Business Managers

Business managers (more often than not, they are CPA's—certified public accountants) are the guys who handle an artist's money, pay his bills when he's on the road touring, invest his money, project tour income and/or losses, and help out with tax forms.

If you are doing a tour of small clubs around the country grossing $200 a show, you will not need a business manager. However, tour the world for a year and a half, and you will definitely need someone to look after your finances at home. Remember, when the tour ends, you don't want to come home and find your health insurance canceled for non-payment of your monthly bills.

During your absence (meaning you're away from home for a prolonged amount of time), your business manager will deposit your money in a checking account and keep all of your bills up-to-date so that, upon your return, it's business as usual.

How is this done, you ask? No, not with mirrors. Upon your approval, your BM will either have your mail picked up at your house or have it forwarded to his office during your tour. Then, as he continues to receive the money you make from performing, he deposits a pre-approved amount in your checking account to pay your bills and the remainder in your savings account. Remember, you've now given your BM **"power of attorney,"** which means he can endorse and deposit or cash your checks on your behalf.

Business managers are also extremely valuable in plotting the income or loss generated from a tour about to start. They can calculate income vs. expenses and let you know beforehand what the expected monetary outcome will be. This will help determine whether you need to go crying to your label for more tour support.

As with all members of your pro team, it's a good idea to interview potential BMs in person. Find out what their offices look like. Are they organized? Do they have many clients? Who are their clients? Meet with them, and discuss your career. It's just possible you don't need a BM at this point in your career.

Compensation

Business managers, like attorneys, are paid either an hourly fee or a percentage of the artist's gross income—usually 5%. The complexity of your career situation will dictate which way to go.

A long, ongoing project will mean daily work on your finances so that a percentage of your income will, in the end, be cheaper for you than paying an hourly rate. On the other hand, a short-term project that requires just some isolated work here and there would justify hourly payments.

Although your personal manager might suggest the names of some pro business managers, the final decision is always yours. Remember—he's being paid from *your* earnings!

Booking Agents

As a band (or solo artist) begins the long, arduous climb to the top, most of the grueling work must be done by the artists themselves because they are not generating enough money to attract professional involvement. So, the booking of clubs and local performances is usually handled by band members.

However, when the band can attract several hundred fans to its local shows and looks to spread its popularity to neighboring cities and states, a booking agent becomes necessary.

The responsibility of a **booking agent** is to solicit work for the artist—to get the artist gigs in clubs and other venues around the country, or around the world, in some cases. In many states, the personal manager is forbidden by law to get employment for the artist, so a booking agent becomes even more valuable.

How Agents Work

1. Once a booking agent agrees to work with an artist/band, he/she will want to know if the relationship is **exclusive** (meaning the agency represents you everywhere and you have no other agents) or **non-exclusive** (meaning the agency represents you in certain areas only).

2. You will then need to send your agent several dozen press packages complete with CDs, demo tapes, photos, reviews, bios, and videos, if available. This is so he can shop the packages to numerous venues at once. (Send him only two packages, and he can send them out to only two venues—get it?)

3. Discuss with the agent the areas of the country you'd like him to focus on. If you're interested in colleges, clubs, fairs, festivals—just say so.

4. Tell your agent what weeks/months you are available so he's aware of when he can book your act.

5. Be certain that you approve each and every potential gig before the agent signs a contract on your behalf. And yes, always get a copy of the contract before it's signed so you can make changes, if necessary.

6. Discuss the agent's commission. Usually, it will be 10% of the gross being paid to the artist/band, per gig. Sometimes, however, an agent won't bother taking a commission if the pay is below $500 or $1,000 a show. Don't let this one slip through the cracks.

7. Find out how you will be paid for each gig. Is the club handing you a check after the show? If so, has the agency fee been deducted already? Did the club mail the check to the agent in advance? Always make photocopies of your contracts to take with you on the road. This way, you'll know the score and will have proof of it.

8. If you decide to go with multiple, non-exclusive agents, find ones that specialize in booking different sections of the country, and assign each one a specific territory. You don't want three agencies all vying for gigs in Arizona, for example, while the remainder of the country is untapped!

9. Give your agent a designated amount of time to get the job done. Tell him you'll stay with his agency for 90/120 days, and give it a try to see what he can do for you. That's plenty of time to get some gigs if he's really working on your career.

10. Do *not* accept excuses like "I'm really busy, but I'll get to you as soon as possible" or "One of my other acts just released a record, and it's taking a lot of my time." All of these excuses mean the agent is too busy for you. These excuses are not acceptable. Fire those agents, and replace them with ones who do have the time for you!

"Going pro" sometimes means having to make the hard decisions. Make them and move on. Always do what's in the best interest of *your* career.

5 Record Companies

Most artists believe that the sole function of a record company is to sign new talent. Yet, these very same artists don't have a clue as to how these giant conglomerates work. Somehow, new CDs mysteriously appear at record shops the world over. And how they get there is anybody's guess.

The easiest way to understand record companies (or **labels**, as they are known) is to think of them as a combination of a bank, a talent agency, and a manufacturing company—because those are their three basic functions.

As a talent agency, the record company does, indeed, search out and discover new talent via its A&R (artist & repertoire) department.

As a bank, it loans money (most of it is **"recoupable"**—meaning the artist pays it back from his royalties) to the artists for touring, video production, advances, and recording costs to make records.

As a manufacturing company, the label designs the CD artwork, prints it, and manufactures the actual records and tapes that are sold in stores. These, in turn, are placed in stores around the country by distribution companies—called **distributors.**

There are six major distribution companies that distribute product from most of the top (major) record companies in the industry—these are commonly called The Big Six, and they are: BMG, Sony, EMD, Uni/MCA, Polygram, and WEA.

There are also other distribution companies that distribute

product from smaller labels and independent labels. I affectionately refer to them as The Big Indies. They are: RED, Navarre, ADA (Alternative Distribution Alliance), Caroline, and INDI.

The bottom line is that if you are signed to a major record company, you will be distributed by a major distribution company. If you're signed to an indie (smaller label), you're likely to be distributed by one, as well. But before we get all hung up on distribution, lets take a look inside a real record company, shall we?

Inside a Record Company

Most major record labels have twelve primary departments, which all function together (though at varying speeds) to make the label run. The object of a record company is to make a profit by selling records so they can stay in business and make more money by selling more records. Ya follow? About 75%-80% of all worldwide record sales can be attributed to major labels and their subsidiaries—or sub-labels.

Here are the twelve departments of a record company that you should become familiar with, along with some helpful hints about each:

A&R

- Responsible for developing and signing new talent to the label.
- Its staff is very well paid and has a large expense account.
- Be prepared to do lots of traveling as an A&R person.
- One or two mistakes, and you're out on your ass!
- These guys oversee the recording of most albums.
- A&R departments help in the selection of material and producers.
- There are A&R vice presidents, directors, managers, scouts, and reps.
- There is also an A&R administrative department to handle the paperwork.

- Primary job of A&R is to develop talent *already* signed to the label.
- Most A&R guys/gals do *not* accept tapes unless they call you.
- No A&R person will sign an act unless he/she cannot live without them.
- It's very easy for A&R guys to get other A&R gigs at other labels.
- It's almost impossible (unless your manager has power) to have them come to a show to see your band play.
- Never ask an A&R person why he didn't like your tape, because he really doesn't know!
- Most labels have A&R reps specializing in all forms of music—one for pop, rock, R&B, alternative, country, etc.
- A&R is one of the most prestigious, powerful, and volatile jobs in the business. The turnover is incredible: A&R today, gone tomorrow!

Promotion

- Responsible for getting the artist's record on the radio.
- Never ask promotion people how they accomplish this!
- Can you say "payola"?
- One of the most pressure-packed jobs in the industry.
- Promotion person's success can make or break a career.
- Be nice to your local promotion person.
- These people bring the records around to stations across the country.
- They are in-tight with program directors at radio stations.
- They also have large expense accounts and wallets.
- Sometimes, a label president will tell a promotion person which records are priorities and which are not.
- Sometimes, promotion people also bring the new records around to the local trade papers (Radio & Records) and magazines (Billboard, HITS) for reviews.

Marketing

- They create ideas for selling your CDs to record stores and consumers.
- Don't assume they have any imagination—help them out!
- You can never do too much marketing.
- Keep it fresh and tasteful. Controversy is OK.
- A slogan or tag line is very important in identifying your product.

Sales

- Their only responsibility is to get records into the stores.
- Volunteering to do in-store performances/appearances might help.
- Check on them—make sure your CD is in your local stores.
- If you're touring, check stores on the road. Report stores that don't have your record.

Artist Development

- Very few labels now have an artist development department.
- Most labels feel that managers should develop their artists.
- Most managers feel that labels should develop their artists.
- Because of this dilemma, most artists never get developed!

Business Affairs

- The department that handles legal work.
- Does label contracts, foreign licenses, record club deals, etc.
- These guys are "the suits" at the record company.

Product Management

- In charge of coordinating the sales, promotion, and marketing departments so they work as a team. Good luck with that!
- Responsible for scheduling exact dates for CD releases.

Production

- They print your CD covers and do the manufacturing and assembling of covers and records.
- Production department ships the records to the distributors.
- Always check and double check the spelling on CD art.
- Have art department sign-off on all final product.
- Don't rush anything here—it could be costly in the end.
- Deadlines are vital—but nobody ever meets them.

International

- This department coordinates the release of your CD around the world.
- A hit in five to six foreign countries can translate to big international record sales.
- Foreign sales increases your income and your touring base.

Operations

- This department schedules the maintenance of the label's recording studios and general office maintenance.
- Not really important in terms of career development.

Video

- Production, promotion, supervision, and distribution of artist video clips.
- Very important people to know.
- MTV, VH-1, etc. call these guys for video clips.

Publishing

- All labels own and control at least one publishing company in ASCAP and one in BMI.
- These days, selling off half of your publishing for a record deal is not at all a common practice.
- If you do sell your publishing to your label, get paid well for it, and make sure you add a reversion clause so you can get it back one day.

Recording Contracts

Now that you know what happens behind the doors of a record company, you probably want information about how this relates to your career, right? I thought so.

Well, record companies offer new artists record deals. And a record deal means a record contract. And a record contract means lots of legal stuff, which means an attorney who costs money that you don't have. Wow! Was that a run-on sentence, or what?

Since most recording contracts are filled with legal terminology and definitions, I'll make it simple. What follows is a list of pointers to discuss with your attorney. Let him take care of the legal mumbo jumbo while you talk about the real important issues, like:

- How long will this recording contract last? In years? In albums?
- Make sure your contract says the label will actually *release* the record.
- Though it's tough, try to to get a **"three-firm"** deal, guaranteeing three albums to be released—no matter what.
- Although it's always recoupable (meaning you pay it back from the royalties you earn), ask for an artist advance. Say you need to buy new equipment or you need money to plant trees in Israel.
- Tell the label you want an option to buy back your masters at a later date. Then wait for them to stop laughing.
- Any deal longer than seven years is illegal in California—it's considered slavery. Ask Smashing Pumpkins.
- You want at least two videos per CD guaranteed in your contract.
- You want only half of the cost of the videos recoupable and the other half absorbed by the record company.
- Guaranteed tour support money should be written into the deal.

- Take the amount of points they offer you in the deal, and add three to it. Then, settle for one additional point when you negotiate.
- Insist on a choice of record producers.
- Insist on input in selecting the singles off the CD.
- Insist on submitting your own, original cover art work.
- Work out a pre-arranged advertising budget, and put it in writing.
- Try to add an additional budget for an indie publicist to promote the CD. This could cost an extra $3,000 per month.
- Make sure you have "creative control" over everything. Or, at least try!
- Make sure there are no "cross-collateralization" clauses anywhere. Be certain to ask your attorney about this ballbreaker!

Although it's very noble to try for all of these things, you'll probably have to settle for just a few. But at least you will have made the effort.

Another thing to keep in mind is that when dealing with a smaller, indie label, you will not have the luxury of asking for an advance or tour support or videos. Damn, you'll be lucky if they fork over $20,000 to record your album!

And as for that touring thing—be prepared to pile four band members and all of your equipment into the back of a van and take it on the road.

What's that? You want advertising? Get a list of fanzines and give a call to their editors—if you can find them.

Above all else, keep this in mind: Once you sign a recording contract and release an album, you are officially in the bottom of the barrel. Your competition is now every record in release and every track being played on the radio across the country. Plan on spending at least a full year touring the country (and the world if you're lucky) in an effort to promote your product.

On the down side comes this little tidbit of reality—the

rigors of touring are responsible for breaking up most bands. Truth. Laying directly on top of your bass player with a Marshall amplifier on your back while making an 800-mile trip is not a pleasant experience. Sharing a single hotel room with the three other members of your band and a four-man road crew is an experience most people can live without. But you're not most people, are you? You wanna be a rock star, right? You're willing to endure pain, rejection, frustration, embarrassment, hunger, and sexually transmitted diseases all in the name of good ol' rock 'n' roll? Well, aren't you? Hello? Is anybody there?

Don't Do This!

The executives, assistants, and secretaries who work at record companies like to live vicariously through their roster of artists. They like to dream about what it would be like to sleep with Taylor Hanson or tour with Steven Tyler. So when you walk into the label, all decked out in your favorite, fits-like-a-glove, black leather pants (you know, the ones that are so tight everyone can see the outline of your genitals), rest assured that the staff is daydreaming about you, too. Wow! What a great guy! What an amazing lifestyle! They roll out the red carpet, bring you soft drinks, and take your lunch order—all because they are fantasizing about you.

So the last thing you want to do is stroll into the president's office and start bitching about getting more points or more advance money. *You are an artist*—let your manager and/or attorney be the bad guy. It's their job to do that. Once you break character and go from rock star to ballbreaker businessman, you've lost the magic forever.

As an artist, you must always be the nice guy—the friend to the downtrodden and overworked at the office, the hero to the record buyers, and the shiny, white knight to the screaming fans. How do you think millions of avid George Michael fans felt when, for months, all they read about was that their hero would never make another record again? That rather than record, he preferred to spend the next five years in court suing his label? Any wonder then, that when he finally did release a new CD it bombed big time? George Michael (yes, one-time biggest artist in the world) lost the magic. Don't go there.

Names and Numbers

Here's something so plain and simple, you'll wonder why you didn't think of it yourself. This one tip alone is worth the price of this book. Trust me.

Fact: to reach any executive at any company anywhere in the world, you must first speak with his assistant/secretary. Here's the conversation:

[Phone rings.]
Assistant: Good afternoon, Michael Goldstone's office, can I help you?
Caller: Yes, is Michael in?
Assistant: Who's calling, please?
Caller: Joe Blow, personal manager.
Assistant: One moment, Mr. Blow—I'll see if he's in.
[Pause while assistant files her nails.]
Assistant: I'm sorry, Mr. Blow, he's in a meeting now and can't be disturbed. I'll leave a message that you called.
[End of phone call. Results: none!]

Now don't you think that if Michael Goldstone or any other exec went into a meeting that his assistant or secretary would be told immediately? Sure. Don't you think they'd be told to hold his calls? Don't you think he'd say about how long he'd be tied up in that meeting? Sure. So when the assistant puts you on hold to "see if he's in," what she's really saying is, "Who the hell are you? You're not important enough to waste my time! I'm in charge of this desk and phone, and you're not getting through! I have the power to make that decision!"

Now, try this approach and see what happens, OK?

[Phone rings.]
Assistant: Good afternoon, Michael Goldstone's office—can I help you?
Caller: Michele, is that you? This is Joe Blow. I need Michael for just a second, is he in? By the way, congratulations on those three Grammy Awards—that was pretty cool.
Assistant: Oh yeah, we're all still pretty excited.
Caller: Well, you earned them!
Assistant: Thanks. Hang on a second, I'll get him.
Michael: Michael Goldstone here.

Notice the difference in tone and how you're treating the assistant in a friendly, more cordial manner? Notice that in this case you call her by name (familiarity) and make her feel important by including her in the label's Grammy success even though all she did was watch it on TV. This is a sign of respect.

Keep in mind that these assistants and secretaries get bitched at all day long by people who are just as frustrated as they are. They are underpaid and overworked and have no power at all. They are executive gofers. However, they can open the doors or slam them shut in your face. Try to find out something about them so you have something in common when you call—a birthday, a favorite movie, a band. Send them a package of your band and ask for *their* opinion. Invite them down to see your band play live at a local show. Make them feel important as often as possible.

And here's the killer touch that'll make you a friend forever. On her birthday, send her one red rose with a handwritten card thanking her for being so kind to you. She'll die! Of course, if the assistant is a male, you're on your own. But the thought is the same. A little kindness really does go a long way in this business.

6 A&R

The mere mention of the letters A&R is enough to piss off most musicians. Why is that? Clearly, they're nice letters. They're strong and tall. They're easy to read. Maybe it's because all musicians know that A&R is, in reality, only one man's opinion when it comes to signing new talent to labels. And you know what they say about opinions—everybody's got one!

The concept of A&R (artist & repertoire) started way back in the fifties when staff record producers at labels began discovering and then producing new recording artists. Because part of a producer's job was to help with song arrangement and structuring, who better to work with newly-signed talent?

In the sixties, A&R giants such as Ahmet Ertegun, John Hammond, Sr., and Berry Gordy (head of Motown Records) were responsible for the signings of such superstars as Led Zeppelin, Billie Holiday, Bruce Springsteen, Michael Jackson, the Supremes, Bob Dylan, Cream, and dozens of others too numerous to mention.

These legendary record company executives not only sought out new talent the world over, but had the foresight to also develop that talent—a function clearly missing in today's music market.

By comparison, the guy who discovered the Offspring (a band that had its fifteen minutes of fame) is already hiding his head and disavowing any knowledge of his relationship with the forgotten act.

Gene Simmons & Kenny Kerner
I often see Gene and Paul around Los Angeles. In this photo, Gene and I ran into each other at a party for Larry Flynt, I believe. Photo shows the Kiss bassist squeezing my face to make sure it's fresh and ripe.

Most laughed at Buddah Records president Neil Bogart for his string of prepubescent bubblegum hits in the sixties, but truth be known, it earned multiple millions for the label and gave Bogart the reputation of being able to break hit records. This, in part, was one of the reasons he was backed by Warner Brothers and was able to start Casablanca Records and sign Kiss. Lucky for me, 'cause I produced them.

Makin' Records

Though the names and the faces have changed over the years, the responsibilities of the record company A&R departments haven't. Contrary to popular belief, the main job of A&R is *not* to spend seven nights a week in dark, smoke-filled clubs seeking out the "next big thing." It's to develop and make records with the artists that have already been signed and have received advances and recording budgets.

When new talent is signed to a label by an A&R rep, that rep becomes the artist's guide and slides him or her through the recording process, which includes selecting a producer, choosing the material, finding a suitable recording studio, coming up with an appropriate budget, and so on, until the CD is completed to everyone's (especially the label's) satisfaction.

Many times, the artist falls short in writing what the label considers "hit material," and the A&R person then sets up meetings with publishers to find hit songs written by outside sources. Sometimes, the A&R rep will hook the artist up with a writing collaborator in hopes of their union producing a hit.

Though they both have long, lucrative careers, Rod Stewart and Michael Bolton have, for decades, recorded hits with outside material.

At times, a new artist will deliberately choose to record an old favorite, hoping that radio will find favor with their new rendition and give it a few extra spins. A&R is integral in the selection and approval of these songs, as well.

Here's a list of ten contemporary artists who covered material by artists from the fifties and sixties:

Ugly Kid Joe	"Cat's in the Cradle" by Harry Chapin
Rod Stewart	"Having a Party" by Sam Cooke
Michael Bolton	"To Love Somebody" by the Bee Gees
Mariah Carey	"Without You" by Nilsson
David Lee Roth	"California Girls" by the Beach Boys
John Mellencamp	"Wild Night" by Van Morrison
Urge Overkill	"Girl, You'll Be a Woman Soon" by Neil Diamond
Alan Jackson	"Summertime Blues" by Eddie Cochran
Mötley Crüe	"Smokin' in the Boys Room" by Brownsville Station
Van Halen	"You Really Got Me" by the Kinks

Before each of these songs was recorded, the approval of the label's A&R department was sought. Remember that your A&R rep is your champion at the record company. He is the person who put his ass on the line for you. He's risking his job and his reputation on your ability to sell records. So work with him, will ya?

Knowledge Is Good

To really be effective at A&R, one needs a deep knowledge of the music business and especially of songs. If you're in your mid twenties, and you can only go as far back as Ratt and REO Speedwagon, you're in big trouble.

It's important to study the roots of rock 'n' roll—to know, for example, that Bow Wow Wow's remake of the classic pop hit "I Want Candy" was originally recorded by the Strangeloves and was based on a rhythm created by blues great Bo Diddley. Or that the Beatles classic love ballad "Till There Was You" was not an original Lennon/McCartney song, but rather a song from the soundtrack of *The Music Man.*

Why is this information important? Because, as an A&R person, it gives you more ammunition—more places to search for material, more catalogs of past hits and obscure releases. It makes you more intelligent and better than the next A&R guy who is also looking for material. It gives you the edge.

Don't Call Us . . .

The down side of A&R is that almost the entire A&R community is virtually inaccessible to unsigned artists and those not working within the industry itself. Additionally, they do not accept **unsolicited** demo packages. "Unsolicited" simply means that the A&R person himself did not ask you to send him the package.

Consider, if you will, the number of artists and bands rehearsing in garages all over the world. Now imagine that each band sends just one demo package to every A&R person at every major record company. Can you say "buried alive"! If the A&R person lived ten lifetimes and did nothing all day and night but listen to tapes, he'd still never get through them all.

Therefore, the best way to make contact is through someone already in the biz—a manager, publisher, journalist, promoter, agent, club owner/booker, record store manager, radio personality, etc. There's usually someone you can think of who's connected to someone who's connected to the industry. And if you want it badly enough, you'll find him.

Now just because you find someone who's able to sneak a package through to the A&R department, don't for a second believe that your phone will ring the next day. Unless you're a mega-manager with a supergroup on your roster, and plenty of power to wield, be prepared to wait up to four months before hearing anything. And then, you'll probably receive a form letter in the mail with absolutely no criticism of your songs. Something very warm and touching like:

> Dear Artist:
> Thank you for your recent submission. Unfortunately, at this time, we are not looking for the kind of material you sent. We appreciate you thinking of us, and good luck with your career.

Sincerely,
Elektra Records
A&R Division

Pretty damn heartfelt, right? Kinda makes you wanna puke, don't it? You would think that, in the four months it took for them to listen to two minutes of your tape, at least they could send back a form letter with some constructive criticism—even if it is checked off. Let's have them tell you a little something about the song structure or the melodies or the rhyme.

Oh, well, maybe in some more perfect parallel universe, but not here!

Decisions, Decisions

During the fifties and early sixties, deciding on new talent was a lot easier than it is today. A&R scouts heard a great voice, and whether or not the artist wrote his own material, that voice was enough to make a deal. Frank Sinatra, Tony Bennett, Nat King Cole, Dinah Washington, Aretha Franklin, and dozens of other great singers and song stylists were signed because of their pipes. The songs themselves could come from publishers and other professional songwriters.

But then, on January 25th, 1964, something happened that forever changed the way A&R worked. On that very date, a single called "I Want to Hold Your Hand" by a new British quartet called the Beatles, hit the #1 spot on the Billboard charts. And believe it or not, it made possible the latter-day signings of such acts as Hanson, David & Shaun Cassidy, Spice Girls, the Monkees, the Romantics, Tiffany, Menudo, New Kids on the Block, the Ramones, the Go-Gos, and Prince, to name just a few.

By topping the charts, the Beatles proved, for the first time ever, that musicians could both write and perform their own material and be successful at sustaining a career—and that image was indeed responsible for record sales if marketed properly. Whether it's torn jeans, an all-girl band, or wearing suits with Nehru jackets, *image* sells records.

That in itself created a dilemma for the A&R community that is still perplexing. Since 1964, A&R vice presidents, directors, managers, and lowly reps have been wrestling with the question of "art vs. commerce." Whether 'tis nobler to sign an artist who will need years to develop a following, radio play, and record sales (Harry Chapin, Tracy Chapman, and Randy Newman come to mind) *or* to go for the immediate hit (Hanson, Spice Girls, Jewel) knowing that the longevity of these artists-with-image, might only be three to five years. Me? I go for the immediate hit—every time. Isn't that the object of a record company? To sell millions of records and have tons of hits? Sure it is!

I believe that a great, fresh, original image/look, combined with great songs, can only help sell records, expose the artist, and build a strong following. So, when I scour the country looking for new bands to manage, I specify that I want young, good-looking teenagers who are hungry, aggressive, and have something special to offer in addition to being able to play and write. Realistically, I want to sell as much merchandise as records.

A&R reps also look for young players. As a musician gets into his late twenties and early thirties, he tends to let the frustration of the industry overtake him. He gets jaded. He focuses more on his day job and his boyfriend/girlfriend relationship. He tends not to believe people because he feels he's already heard it all before. He thinks he knows all the answers. It's not new anymore. The vitality and hunger are gone.

Ever wonder why it takes so long to actually *sign* a deal after an A&R person welcomes you to the label? He wants to check you out. See what problems may arise. Find out if there's a drug problem in the band. Learn who the troublemakers are. If he's gonna put his ass on the line, he wants to be sure you will, too! And for the right reasons.

Kerner's Klass

I remember my thoughts when I first took a look at the original Kiss publicity photo that I found with their demo tape. The word "gimmick" never entered my mind. I swear. I thought it looked so cool. I said, "Yeah—fans are gonna love this. It's totally different. It's controversial. It's new." And it was.

So while a handful of people "got it" immediately and turned Kiss into international superstars, the rest of the world argued about the image. We laughed all the way to the bank. Some thirty years later, we're still laughing, and they're still arguing. Kiss knew all along that they were in the entertainment business and that their jobs were to provide music and enjoyment to their fans as best they could.

We're into the new millennium, and the A&R community is still afraid of bands with images. For the most part (with the exception of a scant few), the community doesn't "get it." They think that image is an excuse for poor material. (The Beatles, the Rolling Stones—poor material?) I think that if a band has an *incredible* image and the material is mediocre, you can always get great songs and give the act time to develop its songwriting craft. Publishers will be knocking your door down to give you their latest potential hits.

If the Hanson brothers were all twenty-six when they released "Mmm Bop," would it have been a huge hit? If women didn't find Michael Bolton incredibly attractive (personally, I don't get this one, but what the hell), would his voice alone have catapulted him to stardom? If the Spice Girls wore dresses and skirts, would they have become mega-stars? No way, Jose. The combination of a killer image (properly marketed) and exceptional material (whether written by the band or acquired from other sources) is usually a winning formula—but *only* to a record company with a vision.

Keep in mind that this is not a new concept. Fans also screamed for the likes of Frank Sinatra, Paul Anka, Bobby Darin, Fabian, Frankie Avalon, Annette Funicello, and a young child star named Michael Jackson. Remember Stevie Wonder when he was Little Stevie Wonder performing "Fingertips, Part Two"? And tell me that you didn't *wet* your seat every time a young Paul McCartney shook his mop-top!

Kenny's Kids

Considering all of the success I've had in discovering new bands, developing talent, and finding great songs for artists, I could never be an A&R person. A manager, yes. A record label president, yes. But A&R, no. Simply put, I don't want anyone second-guessing my opinions on talent. My opinion is as correct as anyone else's. Is John Kalodner right more times than I am? For every act he brings to a label that succeeds, there are probably three or four that bomb, big time. But he never seems to talk about them. And the same is true of every single A&R guy in the business. Because it takes one huge band to rake in millions, labels tend to forgive and forget when it comes to failure. So, it's OK to have four failures if the fifth act you sign is Nirvana. Because Nirvana's success will pay the label back the money it lost on your four disasters.

It's OK for Arista Records president Clive Davis to spend about a million dollars trying to break the Bogmen (unsuccessfully, I might add), because the next Whitney Houston CD will make back the lost money and then some. See how this works? The hit acts make it possible for A&R to sign new acts.

The last thing I need in my life is some twenty-year-old college graduate A&R rep telling me that a band I believe in doesn't meet his standards. What a joke! His entire career will probably be summed up with the signing of two alternative bands that, combined, sold 10,000 records but were the darlings of college radio.

When I find a band that makes me jump out of my chair and react, I couldn't give a damn about labels or A&R. I could care less about what kind of music A&R is looking for or, for that matter, what music is in vogue at the time. When I find a band that truly knocks me out, I want that band. Some of the bands I've worked with—either managing or befriending or

Cartoon Boyfriend
During my almost thirty years in the music business, I've had the opportunity to manage many new bands from around the country. Without a doubt, Cartoon Boyfriend is the most talented I've ever worked with. They are young, aggressive, educated in the ways of the industry, knowledgeable in performing and songwriting, and have an amazingly marketable image. From left to right, they are: Boi, Holly Wright, Tommi Tillman, and Chip Provart.

advising—have gone on to great success, while others broke up and self-destructed. Brunette, Black Cherry, J.T. Harding, Trixter, Poison, Slaughter, Skid Row—some are familiar and others, not. Yet each had something more than material to offer audiences.

If you don't mind, I'd like to spend some time telling you about a band I discovered in 1996 called Cartoon Boyfriend. Why am I asking you? This is my book, remember! Anyway, this story combines elements of management and A&R and the industry in action—so grab some buttered popcorn and a beer and hurry right back.

Cartoon Boyfriend

This is a pure pop band from Los Angeles that I started working with in the spring of 1996. Amidst a plethora of alternative bands sweeping through the airwaves and concert halls, I fell head over heels for a pop band! As an A&R person, I wouldn't even be allowed to consider working with a band that wasn't in some way related to the flavor of the month—unless I brought a note from psychic Jean Dixon!

Songwise, the band was not focused at all. Their material had strong hooks but they were surrounded by lots of unnecessary parts. After about two months of stripping away the fat, the band (who had incredible vocals—all four members sang in every song) came up with a very impressive set of pop fare. Still, the market was decidedly "alternative."

With a very strong teen image (each band member wore a specific color outfit—blue, black, red, and green, to identify his character on stage), blatant good looks, and a cool set of pop songs, the band hit the club circuit. Not surprisingly, they found it difficult to get booked in clubs because most wanted alternative acts. [Note: This problem does not concern an A&R rep.]

The band and I met, and we decided to take gigs at whatever clubs would have us and make a stand at those venues. As we continued to play those clubs, the audiences grew and grew, and eventually other venues in town wanted the band as well.

We were still concerned about playing pop music in an alternative world but were true to our strengths and beliefs and kept going.

All of a sudden, we noticed something strange happening. A young good-looking sixteen-year-old named Jonny Lang was picking up lots of momentum with his live shows. Radio was abuzz with this all-female vocal group called Spice Girls, and the entire industry was waiting for the debut from a brother act called Hanson. The tide had finally turned. Because of their talents and perseverance, Cartoon Boyfriend was now drawing hundreds upon hundreds of people to their shows—ultimately becoming one of the most popular and biggest drawing acts in L.A. It was suddenly "cool" to be in a pop band.

As a manager, I could inspire the band to be true to its music regardless of what was popular at the time. As an A&R person, I have to inform the band that radio is not playing pop so why bother making a record now. See the difference? I could never get the approval to sign a band to a recording deal and then wait two years to develop them and hope their music starts getting radio play again. As a member of the A&R team, I would be out-voted.

Because personal management and A&R must always interface, I must be objective and be sure my bands are in top form and have excellent material. But at the same time, I'm a member of *their* team and must sell the record company on the goods that we have, whether in vogue or not.

Who's to say that we're not gonna be the ones to make pop music *pop*-ular again? I'm sure everyone laughed at The Knack when Capitol released "My Sharona" amidst a blitz of dance/disco music. And Mercury didn't seem to listen when they released "Mmm Bop" in the face of an alternative music market. Incidentally, sixteen-year-old Jonny Lang's debut CD for A&M is platinum!

In all fairness to A&R, it's difficult for them to make a signing when they know full well that it's gonna take over a year from when the ink dries on the contract to the day the CD hits the stores. After all, how can they know what music radio will be playing or what consumers will be buying a year from today? And therein lies madness!

This then should give you some insight into the plight of the lonely A&R rep in his never-ending search to discover new, original talent. One hit signing and you are forever the hero; one big miss and you're out of a job. Well, punk, do you feel lucky?

Why Your Tapes Get Trashed

Although the A&R reps usually listen to tapes that they've called for, many of them wind up in the trash pile simply because they did not adhere to a certain format. A survey of A&R revealed that your tape might wind up in the garbage for the following reasons:

1. Shotgunning (sending tapes out to every A&R person at every label).
2. Simple lack of talent.
3. Terrible-sounding tape.
4. Tape not rewound. (Remember: be kind, rewind!)
5. Sent video and not audio tape.
6. Band has no representation.
7. Tape was really lost in mail.
8. Tape has no number or contact name on it.
9. Too many songs or styles.
10. No follow-up by a pro to get A&R comments.

Here are some important tips to follow *before* you send out your tape:

- Limit your tape to three songs.
- Always rewind your tape to the beginning of first song.
- Always put your best song first.
- Call label to get correct spelling of A&R person's name.
- Listen back to a part of tape to be sure it was recorded properly.
- Put contact name and phone number on case, tape, and J-card.

The Three A&R Deals

There are three kinds of deals an A&R person can make with a new artist: a recording deal, a development deal, or a demo deal. Here are the conditions for each:

Recording Deal

- If the artist has plenty of excellent material.
- If the artist is well-rehearsed and ready to record.
- If the artist has an exciting live show.
- If the artist is focused.
- If the entire A&R department and label execs approve.

Development Deal

This deal usually stipulates that for a predetermined amount of time— usually three to six months—the A&R person himself will work to develop the band and its material so it's ready to record. During this period, artists are forbidden to pitch their material to other labels.

This sounds great but doesn't usually pan out because A&R people are always traveling or in the studio and seldom have three to six months to devote to development. So, even though they mean well, be careful of this one.

Demo Deal

- A&R person hears something special, but artist tapes are poor.
- A&R person wants to record some new, great songs just written.
- A&R person puts band into studio and will spend about $3500.
- Band records 3–5 songs, and label has first rights of refusal.
- If label passes, band can take demos to other labels.

For all practical purposes, next to actually getting signed, this deal best suits the artist. Firstly, the label is spending money to make a professional demo. Secondly, it is recording just the songs the label feels are great. Thirdly, the company gets 45-60 days to decide if they want to sign the band. Lastly, if the label passes, the band comes away with a great-sounding tape that someone else paid for.

Signing Ingredients

One of the most difficult things to understand is what the A&R community is really looking for. What does an artist have to have in order to get signed? For lack of a better name, I call these intangible things "signing ingredients." And the more of them you have, the more likely you are to get signed. During my years as an editor and music journalist, I've had the privilege of interviewing over 200 members of the A&R community and, based on those intervioews, was able to compile a Top 10 list of important signing ingredients. So, in order of their importance, here's what you need to get a deal:

1. Passion

That intangible, inner-emotion a singer or band possesses that makes him/them believable. Otis Redding, Janis Joplin, Aretha Franklin—all possess it.

2. Songs

The very essence of success. The reason this did not come in at #1 is that songs can come from many different places—publishers, covers of other songs, collaborations, etc.—not necessarily from the artist himself.

3. Live Show

This is how a musician sells his CDs and merchandise. A poor live show, and you turn off your audience. A great live show, and you've made a fan for life. Live shows also tell an A&R person whether you are communicating with your audience and if they are accepting your music.

4. Star Quality

Is there someone bigger than life in your band? A Gene Simmons? A Mick Jagger? Someone the fans are drawn to even before the band is signed? Skid Row's lead singer Sebastian Bach had star quality. Remember him?

5. Marketability

Can your image and music be marketed to a targeted audience? Who is likely to buy it and why? There is little demand for Lithuanian accordion music, so regardless of how you shine on that instrument, the chances of you landing a big-bucks record deal are slim, at best.

6. Group Focus

For a solo artist or duo, this is a no-brainer. But, as a band, is everyone pulling in the same direction? Does the band/artist have a plan? Is the manager aligned with the artist? Where are the trouble spots?

7. Hunger

How hungry is this band or artist? Are they spoiled? Will they do anything to be successful? Do they think everyone owes them a deal? Are they willing to earn this deal?

Many artists who have been around for years are under the misconception that because they're still playing and staying together, they have earned the right to be signed. Not true.

8. Business Savvy

Do they know how things work? What kind of "pro team" have they assembled? Do they need a manager? Attorney? What? What do they expect?

9. Red Flags

Are there any troublemakers in the band? Any personal problems? Sex? Drugs? Money problems? Any potential problems beginning to rear their ugly heads?

10. A&R Instinct

What does my A&R gut-feeling tell me? Am I in love with this band? Can I live without signing them? Should I put my job on the line for them? What do others think?

Before making his final decision, an A&R person will see how many of these talent ingredients his act has and go from there. Considering it takes almost one million dollars to break each new act . . . it shouldn't take too long to decide.

The Three A&R Games

Game No. 1

One of the most unpleasant tasks a manager has to face is the in-person meeting with an A&R guy. At the meeting, the manager is supposed to play a tape of his band and expect the A&R guy to both listen to it and make a decision regarding seeing the band live, signing them, or throwing the manager and the tape out of the office. No pressure, right?

I can't tell you how much I despise these meetings. To begin with, whenever I agree to manage a band, it's only because I believe in their talents, their songwriting, and their ability to entertain. I feel that they are destined to become one of the biggest bands in the world, or I don't get involved. Period.

But there I am, handing over a three-song demo tape to a perfect stranger, believing that he will listen through the first chorus and then, as if by wizardry, share my visions for the band! Not likely. Instead, we both sit there uncomfortably and suffer. I suffer because I'm convinced that what I'm handing him has the word "GREAT" written all over it, and he suffers because he cannot commit to anything now. So we play the game: he listens politely and tells me it sounds good but he needs more time. I thank him for his time and leave. And the beat goes on.

Game No. 2

Ever try to get an A&R guy down to a show? What's interesting is that you'll probably get a verbal commitment over the phone, but nobody will actually come down to the performance. Naturally, if you happen to manage a superstar act, labels will roll out the red carpets for you—but handle a local, unsigned artist, and it's like pulling teeth.

Recently, I met with a certain major label vice president of A&R (who shall remain nameless and clueless) at his office. I scheduled an appointment in advance, so I was expected. After shooting the breeze for a few minutes, he played the tape all the way through. All three songs. A good ten to eleven minutes worth of music. When the music was over, he turned to me and asked when he could see the band live. "These are good songs," he said, "Where are they playing next?" He wrote the information down in his appointment book and actually did show up at the club.

The following day, we spoke on the phone, and he gave me his critique of the show. Basically, he liked it. He wanted to hear more. A week later, I followed up with a second demo tape containing three more original songs. After giving him some time to digest the new material, I phoned him again. This time he said that there was "some interesting stuff" on the new tape. More positive reinforcement. All of these positive comments led me to believe that he would continue to follow the band's progress over the next few months. Wrong.

I kept inviting him down to one show after another, one club after another, month after month, each time following up with a reminder phone call and faxes. Nothing. After about three months, he didn't even bother answering the phone. He let his secretary answer and take messages. So here's the question: What do I tell my band? Is this jerk interested or not? If not, why not just say so and stop wasting everyone's time? If he is interested, why not say so and do something?

Game No. 3

The third A&R game can be called "What Do You Think?" because it involves the original A&R person attempting to ask everyone else at his label for an opinion. Here's how it works: If an A&R guy likes your tape, he will ask to see the band live. If he likes what he sees and hears live, he will ask for a second tape with three or four different songs on it. If he likes the second tape, he'll want to see the band live again—just to be sure. Then, when he's sure he wants to proceed, he'll ask other members of his A&R staff to see the act, and he'll ask them for an opinion.

A negative opinion from even one other A&R guy is enough to kill any deal. However, should the posse of A&R reps like the band, the game still isn't over—now, your West Coast A&R guy has to get approval from his East Coast A&R department just to really be on the safe side. And after all is said and done, he'll also want the president of the label to take a look. Remember, it costs close to a million dollars to break every band, so there's nothing like a unanimous opinion to seal a deal.

How to Get It Done, Really

So there you have it—A&R. Before we close this chapter, let me leave you with a checklist of how to really run your career. This is for local, unsigned artists who have local managers. Follow these rules and watch your career move forward:

1. Get your band really tight and ready to play live gigs.
2. Put together a short, thirty-minute "hit-and-run" set of high-powered songs.
3. Put together a simple but classy press kit—don't pack it with useless materials.
4. Line up five or six gigs in your area and a few out of the local club area.
5. Promote every single show as if your career depends on it, 'cause it does!
6. Take names at each show to build a mailing list.
7. *Do not* focus your attention on getting signed.
8. Remember that your job is to play your music in public and entertain people.
9. Have your manager send out 5-6 packages to labels and wait for feedback.
10. After playing out for about six months, begin to invite labels to gigs.
11. Concentrate on drawing more and more fans to your shows.
12. Keep your shows new, fresh, and unpredictable.

13. Send faxes regularly to A&R announcing upcoming shows.
14. After doing this for at least a year, think about releasing an indie single.
15. Market and promote and sell your record at shows and in record stores
16. Try getting some reviews of your record in the music trades and local papers.
17. Add the great reviews to your press package.
18. Fax the great reviews to the labels.
19. Have your manager follow up on first round of packages and send out five more.
20. Try releasing an indie EP or entire CD about five months after the single.

Doing all of this will enable you to develop a large fan following, which in turn will make you a valuable commodity to club bookers and promoters. Your indie records will sell and give you additional money which can be used to further promote your band. The reviews, faxes, and follow-up calls to labels will plant your band's name in their minds, so when they do come down to a show, the club will be packed, fans will be buying your records, and labels will be jealous and wonder why they haven't yet signed you. Then, you've got *them* where you want 'em.

Publishing

Publishing is one of the most lucrative areas of an artist's entire career. For artists and managers who earn publishing commissions, this income is like social security—it lasts much longer than any career and earns income forever. Maybe that's why so few artists are aware of it. Maybe that's why it's such a big secret.

Publishing is all about songs. Period. Because this is such a very complicated area, we'll move slowly, and I'll only give you the basics of publishing so you won't get ripped off.

Copyrights

Before we begin talking in detail about publishing, we need to discuss copyrights for a bit. A **copyright** (defined as a "limited duration monopoly") is like the pink slip for your car; it's basically ownership papers for your songs. A copyright gives its creators limited exclusive rights: the right to perform the work in public, the right to reproduce the work, the right to display the work in public, the right to create a derivative work, and the right to distribute the work.

Songs, whether written alone or jointly with another writer or writers, are copyrightable when they are **original** and in a tangible form. There is no set length in determining what is copyrightable. It could be a six-minute version of Bob Dylan's "Like a Rolling Stone" or the three notes that designate the NBC-TV broadcasting company. When dealing with songs (words and music), **tangible** means that you've written the song down on paper and, hopefully, made a tape recording of it. Singing the song over and over again in the shower does not give you a copyright—although it makes you very clean!

But Kenny, I thought that I had to file a Form PA and mail it to the U.S. Copyright Office in Washington, D.C. to get a copyright. And my friends told me that I should put a copy of the tape and lyrics in an envelope and mail it to myself but not to open the package when it is delivered. What do I do?

The only reason people resort to these tactics is to get an official to stamp a date and time on their creation in the event they need to prove something in a court of law. The copyright office stamps a number and a date on your application, but they do not listen to your tape and compare it to the millions of others to see if you stole your song or infringed on someone else's rights.

If you insist on filing with the U.S. Copyright Office, take a series of your songs (put eight or ten of them on a single tape), and give them a collective name, like *Kenny Kerner's Greatest Hits, 1999*. Then, file the songs as a collection for the same $20 fee! (If you file separately, it's $20 per song. Get it?)

Copyright law states that your copyright lasts for the life of the author plus seventy years. That explains what we mean by "limited" duration monopoly. In case you're writing a song jointly, with another writer, it lasts the life of the longer surviving author plus fifty years. Once your copyright expires, it becomes **public domain,** which means that anyone can use it for free. But I wouldn't worry—by that time, you'd probably be about 130 years old!

Sometimes, you will agree to write a song and not own the copyright. This usually happens when you are creating a **work for hire.** When someone (usually a company) hires you to create a specific work and gives you specific instructions and direction and even oversees the work, that person and/or company owns the work entirely.

All you get is your fee for creating it and usually a writer royalty. This usually occurs when a film company hires a writer to create a theme song or featured song for a movie on a one-time only basis.

Now that you have a basic but working knowledge of copyrights, we can move along into the dark, nebulous world of music publishing. Come along, won't you?

Mechanical vs. Performance Royalties

As writers, you are paid whenever your song is sold on a record and whenever it is performed in public—radio, concerts, TV commercials, jukeboxes,etc. As the owner of the copyright and the writer or co-writer of the song, you (like recording artists) receive royalties. The royalties you receive from your song when it appears on records that are sold are called **mechanical royalties.** They are paid by the record company. The royalties you receive from your song when it is performed in public are called **performance royalties** and are paid directly to you through one of the three performing rights organizations with which you must affiliate—ASCAP, BMI, or SESAC. That's a mouthful—let's take a breather!

You see, the entire concept of publishing is based on the fact that, as a writer, you are a creative person. But your desire to have your songs make money for you necessitates you become a business person as well. Publishers feed on this. They tell you that with their business savvy and your creativity, you can make millions.

The publisher tells you that if you assign the copyright of your song over to him, he will take care of administering all of the business for you—getting other people to record your songs, issuing the proper licenses, doing all of the paperwork, and the collection and payment of royalties.

For handling all of these chores, the publisher usually splits the monetary income 50/50: The publisher's 50% is called the "publisher's share" and the writer's 50% is called, oddly enough, the "writer's share"! Who said there were no geniuses in the music business?

How It Works

One of the publisher's jobs (if he wants to earn his money, that is) is to issue licenses (grant permission) to record companies. For every record that the company manufactures and distributes, it must pay the publisher a predetermined amount of money—literally, pennies. These pennies are the mechanical royalties (also called **"the publishing"**) and the publisher splits them with the writer's/band's publishing company.

Although most bands have but one or two writers, it's often a good idea to form a publishing company and split the writer's share of the mechanical royalties equally amongst all band members. Check this out: If someone gives you half (50%) of an apple, then that half an apple really represents 100% of all the apple you have! Therefore, your 50% of the publishing money represents 100% of your publishing, which you can now split 4–5 ways depending on the number of players in your band. This means that, with a four-piece band, each member can get 25% of the publishing. Though the writers are giving away some money that they've earned, it makes everyone in the band pretty equal. Keep in mind that although Paul Stanley and Gene Simmons wrote most of the Kiss tunes, it was drummer Peter Criss who wrote and sang "Beth," their biggest hit ever.

The money that is due to the writers when their songs are played on jukeboxes, radio, TV, and in films are the performance royalties (also called the **writer's royalties**) and are paid directly to the writers by ASCAP, BMI, or SESAC, who tally the performances from logs kept by the various stations. These royalties are almost never split with anyone other than the actual writers of the songs. *No share of the writer royalties goes to the publisher, either. This is holy money!*

Start Your Own Publishing Company

Artists who plan on releasing their own CDs should start their own publishing companies. To do so, you must decide to affiliate (join) as both a writer and a publisher. First decide on which performing rights organization you'd like to join. I've been in this business for thirty years, and I still can't find anyone who can tell me the difference between ASCAP and BMI—other than that ASCAP is run by writers and BMI by broadcasters. So??? As a publisher, you may have different publishing companies in the different organizations, but as a writer, you can affiliate with only one.

Then, simply call up the PRO of your choice and ask them to mail you both a writer and publisher affiliation kit. They're free and easy to fill out. The most difficult part is deciding on a choice of three names should your first choice for a publishing company name not clear. Oh, yeah, after you release your CD, be sure to notify your PRO so they can track it. Remember, it's up to you to let everyone know that your record is out.

There are all sorts of other publishing terms you will run into as your career develops—terms such as split publishing, co-publishing, sub-publishing, one-off deals, cross collateralization, and reversion—but we'll stick with a basic, working knowledge for now.

The most important thing to remember is this: Always try to keep 100% of your publishing. If you absolutely must sell some off, never give up more than 50%—and make sure you get something valuable for it.

Many artists who are frustrated and in desperate need of money look to their publishing as "the golden goose." If they can sell off half of it for a few thousand dollars now, it'll give them some money to live on for the time being. What they do not realize is that the 50% of their publishing that they sold for a measly $15,000 now, could easily be worth ten times that amount once that same artist is signed and releases a record. Therefore, my advice is plain and simple: if you need extra money—get a job. Do not sell off your publishing!

Also, consider this: once you own your own publishing companies, even if they earn only a pittance, you have a valuable business asset to build on—an asset that will allow you to take out bank loans and use as collateral. So don't be too hasty to cut it loose. Remember that although you fancy yourself a guitarist or singer, you must always run your career like a real business. Because it is one!

Hang On to Your Songs

We're all well aware of the fact that an artist's career lasts between three to five years. Don't bother giving me the handful of exceptions. Once the flavor of the month changes, it's almost impossible to rekindle the bond between artist and fan. So you need to look upon your publishing and writer royalties as the gift that keeps on giving.

I am still receiving royalties from BMI for songs I wrote in the early 1970s. Man, how I wish they were hits! Can you imagine what Lennon & McCartney earned for "Yesterday"? Or Paul Simon for "Bridge over Troubled Water"? Or Lerner & Loewe for their brilliant soundtrack to *My Fair Lady*? Can you say "Show me the money!!!"? Can you say "financial security"???

This should be reason enough for you to hang on to your publishing.

MUSIC PUBLISHERS

by John Braheny

John Braheny

John Braheny is the author of the best-selling Writer's Digest book The Craft and Business of Songwriting *and has conducted songwriting/music-business seminars for colleges, universities, and organizations throughout the U.S. and Canada. Braheny was cofounder/director of the Los Angeles Songwriters Showcase (LASS), a national nonprofit service organization for songwriters, from 1971 until joining forces with National Academy of Songwriters in 1996. He is a past president of the California Copyright Conference, member of the Board of Governors of the Los Angeles Chapter of National Academy of Recording Arts and Sciences (the GRAMMY™ organization) and the National Academy of Songwriters.*

John is an independent consultant for songwriters, performers, and the music industry and can be reached at 818-509-2996 or by e-mail at nutunes@aol.com. He graciously agreed to contribute this material to Going Pro *in an effort to further educate our readers. When it comes to songwriting and publishing, John is "da bomb"! Thanks, J.B.*

I often hear writers and writer-performers say, "I'll never give up my publishing for anything, man. Those guys are just out to rip you off." It's an ignorant and possibly self-defeating attitude. A better statement would be, "I'm not giving up any of my publishing *unless* it's for something I need." Both statements acknowledge that the ownership of a money-making copyright can be extremely valuable. When I question these people, I often find a complete misunderstanding about how this works. Some even tell me that if they give up their publishing, they won't get a dime or credit for writing the song. Wrong! Why would anyone ever want to do that? In a standard single-song agreement, you give up the ownership of the song (unless you share ownership of the song via a co-publishing agreement) in exchange for the services listed below. The traditional split is 50/50. (There is no law that dictates it.) A point of negotiation is whether or not costs of collection and other administration expenses (usually 15%) should come off the top *before* the 50/50 split.

If we look at the total income as 200%, as they do on ASCAP and BMI clearance forms (the forms you send them to let them know that you or someone else has released your song on a recording), 100% is called the writer's income (divided by the number of writers on the song), and the other 100% is the publisher's income, usually referred to as "the publishing" which also may be split. *Do not, under any circumstances, sign away your writer's royalties.*

You may be able to negotiate a contract for part of "the publishing," if: a) you're a successful recording artist or writer, b) the publisher is excited enough about your songs, c) the publisher is in competition with other publishers for your songs, or d) you can convince him/her that you'll personally be very aggressive about pitching the tune to producers and artists yourself.

So, what do publishers *do* to earn their take? The two major functions a publisher performs are 1) exploiting your material and 2) collecting your money. Exploiting your music means getting it used via records, films, TV, music boxes, video games, MIDI files, greeting cards, commercials, sheet music, and anything else their and your creativity can come up with. Collecting royalties from all those sources is self-explanatory, though doing it thoroughly is seldom a simple task.

Here are a few things you should know about publishers and publishing:

Getting a song published doesn't mean anything. Getting a song recorded often doesn't either.

Wide-eyed amateurs can frequently be heard saying "I just want to get a song published," but other than proving to a spouse or parent that all that demo money they spent may not have been in vain, it's really not worth much unless the song actually generates income.

It's not like getting a book published. If you look closely at your contract, you'll discover that nowhere does it promise they'll get your song recorded. In fact, if they do, you should be suspicious. They can't guarantee anything because even with a great song, they can pitch it a hundred times, get it put on "hold" numerous times, and it still might not get recorded. Even if it does, there's no guarantee that it will be released. And even if it's released, there's no guarantee it will sell enough records to let you quit your day job.

Even if you get a song published or get an exclusive staff-writing deal, you must keep pitching your songs.

It's so tough to get songs recorded these days that publishers rely on writers to use their own personal contacts to secure recordings of their songs. In fact, I'd venture to say that most exclusive "staff-writing" deals today are the result of an astute publisher recognizing that a writer has ended up on the charts with a song he/she self-publishes, then investigates to find that the writer is part of a circle or clique of writers or writer/producers who are generating their own projects. This happens primarily in pop, rock, and R&B and not so much in country. However, even in country, the ability of the writer to network, perform on showcases, and otherwise expose their songs to artists and producers is definitely a consideration in signing. The point is, if you get a song published, you can't just sit back and figure that the publisher will do all the work and always consider your song for pitching situations, particularly at a major company with a huge catalog.

So, you might ask "What's the point in having a publisher if you still have to pitch your own songs?" The answer is that two heads are always better than one and that a substantial part of a publisher's job is done after the song is placed by making sure you (and the publisher) collect all the money you're due and to find additional uses for the song once it has achieved some exposure (commercials, film and TV, etc.).

Publishers can turn down deals, and you'll never know about it.

You're sleeping in your car and wondering where your next meal is coming from. Meanwhile, a song you had published is up for inclusion in a film, and the budget is big. Your publisher is negotiating the **synch license** and is out to pull off a deal that will make you both a lot of money. If he succeeds, he'll be a hero, if not, you both lose—but you'll never know it. You don't know this is going on because you haven't bothered to check in. As it happens, your publisher overbids what he's asking for the song, and the film company decides against it. Had he not been such a hard-nose about it, you could have moved out of your car and eaten well for years on 50% of what he turned down. This may seem like an exaggeration, but it has happened.

It also happens that the film company insists on splitting the publishing. Such an agreement wouldn't affect your income much but would definitely affect the publisher's since they'd be giving up a percent of ownership. Major publishing companies will rarely, if ever, make that kind of deal.

The real point of this is that, ideally, you should know your publisher and have a relationship that allows you to feel comfortable about checking in periodically, and that your publisher will let you know if something is going on that will affect your life. Your contract will probably say that your publisher owns the song and can do anything he/she wants with it without getting permission from you. That's a pretty standard clause so it becomes important that you stay in touch.

Don't ever pay a penny to sign a publishing or recording contract.

One of the biggest scams for songwriters and lyricists is perpetrated by people generally referred to as "song sharks." Typically, a **song shark** buys names and addresses of songwriters through a broker who accesses the records of the U.S. Copyright Office to find all those who have recently copyrighted their songs. This is not illegal because the Freedom of Information Act gives Americans access to public documents that are not classified. In fact, successful song sharks are careful to operate within the law and don't promise what they can't deliver. They victimize you by capitalizing on your ignorance and your ego. They make it sound like something you always dreamed of, and your ego allows you to buy it. They give you what they promise, but it isn't anything like your dream. Here's typically what happens:

1. You receive a letter from someone you never heard of, saying that they heard about your song and that if it passes their rigid (yeah, right!) screening process (which they ask you to pay for) you'll be offered:

a) A publishing contract.

b) A recording contract in which your song, produced and arranged by their "experienced staff" (which you will pay for), will be included on a CD that will be distributed to the music industry and sold to the public and/or played on the radio. (Realize that if they sell one record, send the CD to one "industry professional," and/or get the song played at 3 a.m. at a five-watt station in Nebraska that they bought time on, they have fulfilled their contract.)

[Please note: There *are* legitimate compilation producer/distributors who will charge you for inclusion of the recordings you have produced and distribute them to the industry and radio. They include samplers from the music trade journals such as Album Network and College Music Journal (CMJ). However, always check them out carefully by getting copies of previous releases, checking the quality of the material, and calling the artists who appear on the previous compilations. They should list contact numbers; ask the artists if they felt it was worth the money.]

2. You send the song and their fee (or work out a payment plan) with the signed contract, after which:

d) If you've received a publishing contract, frankly, that's where it all ends. That is, unless they own a record company that's part of the publishing company (they will not let you know this), and they are able to secure a recording contract for you or get your song recorded by an artist (who, I will guarantee, you have never heard of) on that record label. There may also be another "fee" for this.

e) You hear an average-to-mediocre performance of your song by a singer who sounds like they've already recorded ten songs that day. It's probably true; it's an assembly-line process. You will never receive royalties because they will never sell enough records to generate royalties.

The rule of thumb is that you *never pay* to have your song published or to get a recording contract. The only person you should have to pay is your attorney.

Every contract is negotiable.

It's easy to be intimidated by a publisher who you feel is answering your dreams and loves your song(s). Don't forget, though, that depending on how badly he needs your song, you may negotiate. Here are some points you can negotiate.

- Get a reversion clause. (See below.)
- Get the publisher to agree to not grant a license for less than the current **statutory mechanical rate**—7.1 cents per song per record/CD/tape sold—without your permission. This rate lasts until the year 2000, at which time there will be an increase.

- Changes in the song are not made without approval of the writer.
- You may want to specify that your song cannot be used for commercials, X-rated films, etc. without your permission, if that's important to you.
- If you made the demo that the publisher uses, make note of the costs, and ask that the publisher returns those costs from the first royalties that are earned by the publisher. You may also ask that you be reimbursed for the demo costs as an advance at the time of signing the contract.
- In the event the publisher wants to bring in a cowriter later, he can't allow that writer or combination of writers to receive more than half your writer's share.
- Regarding sheet music and other print music royalties, try to get 50% of what the publisher gets rather than a penny amount per copy.

Remember, though you should try to negotiate all the above, your ability do it, as always, depends on your negotiating position. Also, never sign anything without the advice of an entertainment attorney.

Never sign a "single-song" contract without a reversion clause.

When a publisher signs a song, they're gambling their money and time invested. Your gamble is that a potentially successful song is kept off the market for the rest of the life of the copyright because the publisher doesn't get it recorded and it sits "on the shelf." Major publishing companies have thousands of songs in their catalogs that are never recorded or recorded only once. They tend to be most active with writers currently on staff. So, what happens when you're not getting the attention? How can you assess the degree of activity a publisher will devote to your song? You can't, so you need a way to protect yourself.

A **reversion clause** in your contract says that, if the publisher fails to get the song recorded or placed in TV shows or films within an agreed time (two years gives the publisher enough time), the contract is canceled and the song is returned (reverts) to the writer. If you see that the publisher continues to actively pitch your song, extend the time period. There are different aspects of the reversion clause you can negotiate: 1) the length of time, 2) that it should revert *automatically* and not depend on your sending notice first, 3) a minimum amount of money the usage should generate before the publisher can keep it, 4) that the song has to be recorded by someone not directly affiliated with the publisher, and 5) that the artist who records it is recently successful. The latter is tough to negotiate unless you're already a successful writer.

Signing a song contract or an exclusive "staff writer" contract with a major publishing company isn't necessarily better than signing with an independent.

A "major" company is one that is owned by the large record labels, film companies, or other entertainment conglomerates. Independents are those without those affiliations and range from single individuals to large well-staffed companies. Regardless, the effectiveness of a publisher gets down to the credibility of the individual, her contacts, access to projects, aggressiveness, and ability to network. When she calls someone about a song she represents, does the person she's calling trust that she'll send or bring a high-quality song appropriate for the project? The other factor is the ability to collect or contract an effective administration company to collect and distribute royalties.

There is one advantage that majors have: cash flow. It allows them to spend more money and take chances an indie may not be able to take. For instance, they can sign writer/artists to development deals, hire a producer to produce masters, hire a publicist, etc. Though some large indies have cash flow, small indies have to rely solely on their creativity and credibility.

Finding a good publisher could be the best move you make.

If you aren't a good salesman for yourself, hate making cold calls and networking, and you aren't a candidate for starting your own publishing company for the songs you write (something you'd want to do if you're an artist or band who records your own songs), chances are you'll want to find someone to represent you. Since there aren't agents for songwriters, you'll be looking for a music publisher. Even if you're a writer/performer or a band, you should consider a **development deal** with a publisher who may be in a position to help launch your career. Typically, it would involve splitting the publishing (giving you 3/4 of the total royalties) and a time limit for the publisher to get you a deal. Getting a song recorded by a major artist has also proven to be a door opener for writer/artist careers, but getting through the doors to those artists requires a set of skills and contacts every successful publisher needs to have. You can invest the time in developing them yourself or invest half of your royalty income to have a publisher do the job.

The above information is only a fraction of what you should know and a fraction of what's available to know, but hopefully, it's enough to keep you out of trouble.

For further information on music publishing, check out John Braheny's book, The Craft and Business of Songwriting, *Randy Poe's* Music Publishing: A Songwriters Guide, *and Todd Brabec and Jeffrey Brabec's* Music, Money and Success.

Songwriting

Nobody can tell you how to write a song, so just forget it. A veteran songwriter can suggest changes or mention some writing tips to a fledgling songwriter, but don't ever try to tell someone how or what to write.

I'm aware that what I just said is contrary to what almost everyone else believes, but I'm here to let you know how it really is out here in the biz. And here, anything that gets you to the top is right. I learned that the hard way. I've written some 300 songs during my career—some were in movies, some were recorded on albums, but none were hits. Not being able to play a single musical instrument (I'm left-handed, and teachers thought I was a freak), my songs come into my head with a finished melody. That's the way God wanted it to be, I guess. I can't just sit down with a pad and pen and start writing a song from scratch.

About fifteen years ago, I was dozing off while watching the farm report on television. Some farmer down south was bragging about his prize pig. "Her name's Ramona," the farmer said, "and when I call, she comes to me." I went to sleep. About six hours later, I awoke, took my pad and pen, which I always keep near the bed for such emergencies, and wrote the following verse, following the melody I heard in my head:

Ramona she comes to me, so crystally clear
Like a star in the skyway, and then disappears
She's crying, she's dying for some kind of peace
Ramona, just do as you please . . .

The following afternoon, my songwriting partner and I finished the song. Even though I think it's one of the best we've written, most likely nobody will ever hear it. That's because songwriting, in addition to being a craft, is also a business. I had the craft and the talent parts together, but I didn't have the time to take care of the business side of it.

About fifteen songs that I co-wrote with another partner were recorded by a rock group called Dust, in the late sixties and early seventies. I also co-wrote a tune with Dominic Frontierie (he's famous, guys), which made it into one of those *Cleopatra Jones* movies. The remainder of the 300 songs I wrote will be left to my son Demian when I die. Unless I change my mind and decide to bulk erase the tapes.

The Golden Rule

Experts will try to tell you that you need to structure a song a certain way, but you don't. For every example they give you, someone can find the exception to that rule. Here's the one rule I came up with that applies to every single hit song and hit record:

You must leave the listener with something to remember.

It could be a giant chorus ("Everything Is Beautiful"), a bizarre song title ("Rainy Day Women #12 and 35"), a catchy, repetitive phrase that has nothing to do with the song's title at all ("Tubthumping")—whatever. If there's something they remember, they'll go out of their way to buy it.

Hit Songs vs. Hit Records

What's that? Why did I purposely make a distinction between a hit *song* and a hit *record*? Aren't they the same thing? Certainly not. See if you can go through the following list and separate the hit songs from the hit records:

1. "Smells Like Teen Spirit"
2. "Bridge Over Troubled Water"
3. "Peaches"

4. "Unforgiven"
5. "Yesterday"
6. "Mmm Bop"
7. "I Could Have Danced All Night"
8. "Everybody's Gone Country"
9. "Till There Was You"
10. "Communication Breakdown"

If you guessed that songs 2, 5, 7, and 9 were the hit songs, you're right. Although all ten songs were big hits according to Billboard magazine, each topping the charts in its own genre, only songs 2, 5, 7, and 9 will live forever. They are classics. They can be heard in elevators, as instrumental versions, on airplanes... The others were big chart hits, but it's unlikely you'll get the London Philharmonic Orchestra to do a cover version of the Presidents of the United States of America's tune "Peaches" or the Wank track "Unforgiven."

Though both hit songs and hit records earn money and fame for their writers and performers, only hit songs live on and are immortal. A thousand years from now, when humans are sitting in their dentist's chair getting their teeth filled with laser guns, the office radio will still be playing Lennon and McCartney's "Yesterday," probably performed by the Interplanetary Digital Community Orchestra. That's the difference.

Don't get me wrong. Don't believe for a second that having a dozen hit records is a bad thing. No, no, no! If all continues to go well for Hanson, they'll be able to retire by the time Isaac reaches twenty years old and Zachary's voice changes.

Observations

Ever since my mom bought me my very first radio, I've been mesmerized by music and made a career of studying it, writing about it, and teaching it. There are some very interesting things about radio and the songs that are played on it. For example, its fascination with records named after girls, like "Donna," "Barbara Ann," "Peggy Sue," "Michelle," "My Sharona," "Oh!

Carol," "Hello Mary Lou," "Sherry," "Beth," etc. Also, songs with numbers in them or ones that name cities in the United States, like "Beechwood 4-5789," "1-2-3-Red Light," "ABC-123," "7&7 Is," "26 Miles," "Engine, Engine #9," "I Would Walk 500 Miles," "Arizona," "Midnight Train to Georgia," "By the Time I Get to Phoenix," "Tallahassee Lassie," "Woodstock," "Mississippi Queen," "I Left My Heart in San Francisco," "Please Come to Boston," "Chicago (My Kind of Town)," "New York, New York," "Detroit City," "Montego Bay," "I Love L.A.," and the classic "Kansas City."

Structural Pointers

You probably thought I was gonna give you another checklist, right? OK, you got me. My idea all along was to give you lots of lists so you'd tear them out and carry them with you, and eventually, you'd have to buy another copy of this book. However, since I'm calling these pointers, they don't count as a checklist. But the information is just as vital:

- Try to avoid clichés and predictable lyrics. The lyrics of a song are as important as the music because they're what most people identify with. Make them clear, cohesive, creative, and new.
- Whatever rhyme pattern you choose for the first verse you should use for every other verse that follows.
- Don't use words that are awkward or that people will have to look up in a dictionary. (Donovan, Gilbert O' Sullivan, and Procol Harum already did this.)
- The lyrics to your chorus should be the same each time the chorus is sung. That way, listeners will remember it and be able to sing it—and ask radio to play it!
- Be yourself. Write only what you feel, when you feel. Don't be influenced by what's on the radio or who's being signed.
- Make sure that your storyline makes sense and is complete. Don't make listeners figure out what you meant to say.

- After finishing a new song, let it sit for a week, then listen to it again with fresh ears. Don't be afraid to change it for the better.

Dummy Lyrics

Most songwriters I know write their lyrics first and then lock into the exact melody. But sometimes, when the melody comes at the same time, you're caught off guard and don't have the exact lyrics you want. To make certain you don't ever lose sight of a good melody, you should immediately write down **dummy lyrics**—lyrics in the same meter as the melody that will help you remember the melody.

When Paul McCartney first wrote the classic Beatles tune "Yesterday," he wrote the words "Scrambled Eggs" down on paper because that phrase also has three syllables (same as "Yesterday") and is sung in the same meter. Then, after the song was locked into place, and he wrote the *real* lyrics, he came up with "Yesterday."

Use dummy lyrics as a tool to help you remember your meter and melody lines.

9 Demos & Press Kits

This is a chapter you might want to tear out of the book and carry with you every day. It talks about the basic presentation requirements for shopping in the music business.

Remember this truth: No artist in the music business can make it through from local, unsigned band-status to inking a record deal without having, at some point, recorded a demo tape and put together a press package. And that's a fact, Jack!

The Demo

So let's start at the beginning, shall we? **Demo** stands for "demonstration." It is a demonstration of your music or your songs. It is not a master quality, final representation—but rather an *indication* of what you can do as writers and musicians. To the A&R community, your demo tape says, "Here, check this out."

A&R reps have heard all kinds of sparsely recorded demo tapes—from piano/voice to a capella. It's all the same to them (especially to those who have no ears). So...

Rule No. 1:
Do not spend a fortune recording your demo.

There are thousands of low-cost demo studios that would die for your business—some charging as little as $100 for an entire song. Considering that a demo tape, ideally, should contain your three best songs, that's a mere $300 for a complete tape to service to the industry.

But we're putting the cart before the horse here. Let's step back a minute and deal with the phrase "three best songs." What are our three best songs? How do we pick them? Who do we ask? Don't you really mean our three *most popular* songs? The songs our fans like the most?

No. I said "best," and I mean best—as in *better than the others*. As in best structure and format. As in strongest chorus. As in best-written, sung, and performed. Are you beginning to understand what "best" means? Good, because that's rule no. 2.

Rule No. 2:
Always choose your three best songs.

Now that you've got it, try this on for size: All three songs should be in the *same* musical genre. Many bands and writers are exceptionally talented and able to write in many different styles. However, to the record companies, this shows a lack of focus. When you're a star, this is called diversity, but when you're unsigned, this same talent is a lack of focus. (Don't ask!) This brings us to rule no. 3 . . .

Rule No. 3:
Stick to a single, specific musical genre.

In other words, don't try to show a label what you might be able to write five years down the road—show them that you can write great songs in a specific musical style *now*. That, alone, makes you worthy of getting signed. Keep in mind that when they listen to your tape, they're also thinking about what market you appeal to, and if they hear conflicting styles, then that translates into conflicting markets for them—which, of course, translates into no deal for you!

Once again, we turn to the Beatles for an example: If the Fab Four had put together a demo tape back in 1963 with "I Want to Hold Your Hand," "She Loves You," and "Thank You Girl," it would have defined their pop/vocal style. However, if that same demo had contained "She Loves You," "Strawberry Fields," and

"Helter Skelter," how would they have been categorized? Pop? Rock? Eclectic? Underground?

What's really funny here is that the music business is built on individuality, yet the A&R community is lost if it can't put a new artist into an already-existing category. Can you say "double standard"?

Choosing Your Best Songs

Finding out which three of your songs are best is going to be a difficult task. Who do you ask? Where do you go? To begin with, never let your fans decide. Firstly, they know little about songs, and secondly, they're likely to think everything you play is great. That's why they're fans, remember!

Try to find someone with more of a musical background—someone connected to someone in the industry, maybe. A personal manager, a publisher, a member of a group on a label, an attorney . . . If all else fails, try a local club owner or college radio DJ or record store manager that you might know. Regardless of where you live, there's someone you can ask. Then, after you give out five tapes, wait for an answer, and see how many choose the same songs as their favorites. That will give you an idea. As it turns out, many times the fan favorites are the band's best. But you'll never know unless you ask around.

Pre-Production and Recording

Now that you know which three songs to record, you may proceed with that process. The first step in the recording process (after song selection) is **pre-production**. This is where you and the band work out the kinks in each of the song and practice rehearsing it with and without vocals—as if you were in the studio. If you plan on recording drums and bass first, rehearse it that way, too.

At pre-production, you will trim the fat from the songs and decide if they will fade out or end cold when recorded. This is one of the most important parts of the process.

If you plan on paying for a recording studio, do not waste time and money working out the parts there. Do it in a cheaper rehearsal studio for far less money. I've seen too many bands set up shop in studios and pay upwards of $150 per hour to rehearse when they could get the same results for $15 an hour at a rehearsal studio. Duh!

It's always a good idea to start shopping for a studio when you begin pre-production. That way, you have a deadline and something to look forward to. If you know you have to begin the actual recording in exactly two weeks, that gives you a set schedule to follow. If you're recording in your home or garage studio, it's still a good idea to schedule things so you have something to work toward—a goal of sorts.

Your first attempt should always be to try and get the studio for free—as a favor from a friend, let's say. Second best is to make a "spec" deal. "Spec" stands for **speculation.** This means that the studio owner believes in the band and the music and will allow you to record for free. (Usually, you still must pay for tape costs.) Then, if you make a deal, you pay him back for what your studio time costs. If you fail to make a deal, he speculated and lost.

Here's your official "spec" checklist:

- Always get the deal in writing.
- Find out who keeps the master tapes until the deal is made.
- Lock into consecutive recording dates. Many spec deals drag on and on.
- Try to find someone to produce your dates.
- Speak with the engineer, and insist he come to rehearsal.
- Make sure the studio owner cannot release the masters to anyone.
- Be specific about your plan. Are you only recording? Or mixing? Or both?
- Are the recording facilities acceptable for mixing?

- What's included in the deal? Extra amps? Mikes? Outboard gear?
- Confirm your actual days and hours of recording.
- Let your engineer know your plan ahead of time so he can prepare the studio before you arrive to record.
- Find out if your spec deal means you have to pay the engineer.
- It's a good idea to occasionally treat the engineer to lunch or dinner.
- If you're mixing at the same studios, be sure to leave with a DAT copy and cassette copies of your songs.
- Don't make *any* deal without seeing and hearing the actual studio you will be using.
- If things are going great, make certain you let the owner know about it.
- Don't waste time. Be serious, but have fun doing it.

Reproducing Your Tapes

Now that the recording and mixing processes are done, you'll need to make copies of your tape. First, find a reputable duplication place by asking around and checking in local music magazines. Compare costs, turnaround time, and other benefits. Find out how many copies you need (then add an extra twenty-five for emergencies that always pop up), and ask where the price break comes.

If you have twenty minutes of recorded music, you don't need a sixty-minute tape, so time the music on your demo, and have that information ready. If you're prepared to order seventy-five tape copies, you might be able to get an extra twenty-five copies for a few dollars more if that's where the price break is. Take advantage of it.

If you have any specific instructions about your tape, let them be known. How "hot" do you want them recorded? What sequence? How much time between songs? What information do you want on the cassette and J-card? *Always make sure there is a contact name and telephone number on both the cassette tape and the J-card.* Nobody is going to check the local Yellow Pages to find you.

Most likely, your tapes will be done within a week. When you pick them up, check them—make sure the spelling and phone numbers are correct. Count them. Do not assume someone already did. Be a pro; take the time to do things right. Too many times, bands walk out the door and start sending out demos with an incorrect telephone number. If the number is off by one digit, you will not be contacted. If there is no area code, you will not be contacted. Don't set yourself up for failure.

It's also a good, professional idea to keep a running list of each person who is getting a press package. You want to make sure they get only one package, and also you'll want to follow up on those mailings.

The Press Kit

In the music business, the folder that contains your photo, bio, press clippings, and demo tape is called your **press kit** or **press package.** The same package goes to record companies, agents, attorneys, and the media. So it better look good and contain everything you need others to know—without giving them a week's worth of reading materials.

When putting together this important package, *less is more.* Too much to read will make someone impatient. And realistically, what can you say about a brand new act that has no real career?

Your press kit should contain the following materials only:

- A clear, crisp, 8x10 photo with artist/band name and contact info.
- One or two short, positive reviews or press clips.
- Lyrics to the three songs on your demo tape (stapled together in the order that they play on the tape).
- A band ID sheet detailing each member's name, age (if under 25), instruments played, and who writes the songs. No need to mention where the band is from

or how long they were together floundering around doing nothing.

- If you have three or four direct quotes from some very reputable people in the business—managers, producers, artists—include them on a separate quote sheet, but be sure to attribute them correctly.
- Include a business card from your manager or representative.
- Don't forget your demo tape or CD, Einstein!
- Always include a cover letter with every package explaining why you're sending it.

That's all, folks. Your aim is to get people to listen to your *music,* not spend the afternoon reading your press materials. Remember this: if you have a giant stack of press materials, you've probably been around for a long time. If that's true, why aren't you signed yet? Must be something wrong. Maybe you're not good! Therefore, *less is more.* Always.

Artist Photos

We need to spend a few minutes talking about the photos you're putting in your press packages. Do they really represent you? Do they somehow depict the kind of music you play? Do they look pro?

I have yet to find a single artist who was incapable of somehow finding a photographer to take a few pictures. Everyone has a relative or friend with a camera. It's up to the artist to be creative. You don't need a thousand-dollar photo session—merely one that looks like it cost a thousand dollars. In other words, make it look good for a few bucks.

Do not, for example, stand in front of a forest so we can't distinguish you from the trees. Do not wear a watch or be photographed in front of a calendar so the photo is dated a week later. Do not stand in front of a black curtain or backdrop wearing all black; you'll come out with a head and no body. Keep it simple.

Try to look like the music you're playing. Don't wear rainbow-colored clothes if you're a metal band—look dark and dirty, like the music. Ozzy Osbourne always looks like his music. There's no mistaking it. The Rolling Stones always look like trouble-making rock 'n' rollers. The Grateful Dead always looked and dressed like hippies on pot. And so did their enormous audience. Remember that you want to help the consumers in identifying you and your music, not confuse them.

Cover Letters

As I mentioned earlier, every single press package that goes out must be accompanied by a cover letter explaining why it was sent. Usually, this letter is written by the artist's manager, attorney, or, in some cases, by the leader of the band himself.

Like everything else in your new press package, this letter should be short, to the point, and very pro. It should explain, in a few paragraphs, who you are, why you sent the package, and what you expect. Here's a sample (albeit short) cover letter:

Kenny Kerner Management
1111 East 11th Street
Suite 1111
Los Angeles, CA. 91111
Telephone / Fax: 310-111-1111

John Doe
Dover Records
3475 Dover Place
Dover, Colorado 78231

May 22, 2001

Dear John:

As the personal manager of the Los Angeles-based rock band BIGFOOT, I have enclosed a complete press package and demo for your perusal.

The band is currently drawing about 200 people per show locally and is being played on WXTB and KKLV in Denver.

I feel their songs are very well-constructed and radio-ready, and value your professional input.

I'll give you a call in a few days to be sure this package arrived. Please don't hesitate to contact me should you need further information. Thanks in advance for your time and consideration.

Sincerely,
Kenny Kerner
BIGFOOT Manager

Six short sentences say it all. Again, you want this person playing the tape and not making paper airplanes out of your press materials.

Following Up

Sometimes it will take months to hear from these people—even with follow-up calls. Don't give up. Don't get frustrated. Remember that they're getting the same kinds of packages from hundreds of other people around the world, and you're probably not at the top of their listening list.

At the very least, you'll be able to reach and speak with an assistant or secretary who'll be able to tell you if your package was received. Almost all labels now log in packages on their computers with a date and name of artist or band.

Make it a friendly call. Ask if her boss plans to listen to the tape and about how long that takes. Make a joke. Make light of the matter. He/she's had a tough day. Ask if you can call back in a few weeks, and you'll be surprised that most will say "yes." Always say "thank you."

After you hang up the phone, make a note in your appointment book to follow up with a second call in about two and a half weeks. Mark down the name of the person you spoke with because you'll want to use it again. There's nothing like a friendly voice on the phone.

What you'll find is that your phone calls will most probably be meaningless and will have had no effect on getting the tape listened to any sooner. But it is good therapy, and it is something you can relay to the band. You've done your job. You followed up.

If your packages were sent out to record companies not accepting unsolicited material, be prepared to get them back unopened, in the mail. Again, it's not personal. You might want to call each label and find out in advance if a particular person is accepting material. If they are, ask if there is a secret code you need to indicate on the outside of the mailing envelope.

An A&R friend of mine accepted packages from others in the industry, but only if the words "Miami Dolphins" were written in the lower left-hand corner of the envelope. That's how he and his assistant identified a solicited package. Naturally, each month, he changed the name of the football team to keep people from catching on.

Another good tip is to send out several press packages and not think the one you mailed out is the one that's gonna get you signed. You might have to send kits to twenty or thirty labels before anyone takes notice.

These kits are also good for soliciting a personal manager, music attorney, agent, club gig, publisher, or just about anything in the biz. To update them, just include a brand new photo every year and change the press clippings occasionally.

10 Self-Promotion

When you're finally signed to a record deal, the label's media relations person will attempt to do publicity for you and your upcoming record. However, burdened with the same chores for about a dozen other acts on the label, the effort will be sincere but the results minimal. So once again, you're left to your own devices and creativity to get to the next level. And trust me, it never stops: GETTING SIGNED MEANS YOU ARE NOW AT THE BOTTOM OF THE BARREL.

Advertising and promotion are essential in any business. If you open a hamburger stand, you need to advertise. If you release a record, you also need to let people know it's out. The chances of them stumbling upon it at their favorite record store are slim, at best.

Because hiring a publicity expert can cost as much as $5,000 a month, plus expenses, let's talk about self-promotion for a bit. Self-promotion is where you promote yourself and your products. And who better? Who knows more about your band or your record than you, yourself? Knowing this, you already have half the battle won. Now, all you need are some bright ideas, a little money, and some good, old-fashioned elbow grease. Shall we begin? OK!

Promote Your Shows

Because most unsigned artists spend more time performing at local gigs than they do in recording studios, promoting your shows properly is a must for building a fan base and creating a buzz. Additionally, if you do not draw well, most clubs won't book you again. And that means it's only a matter of time before you run out of places to play. So to most artists, "promotion = survival" on the club scene.

Like politicians, good promotion always gets down to meeting and greeting—telling the people who you are and where you'll be playing. There's no better place to start than right in the club you'll be playing at in the future. So make it a point to tell the club owner you'll be visiting his club on Friday and/or Saturday nights (when they are most likely to have the largest crowds) to hand out **flyers** and promote your show.

Flyers are relatively inexpensive to print and can be done up at almost any centrally located printing place—Kinko's, Sir Speedy, you name it. Try to find the cheapest place that has the quickest turnover. You don't want to wait three weeks to get your flyers done.

You want to make your flyers small, so people can take them home. Full-sized 8x10 paper is far too large and bulky. Something about the size of a postal card is more appropriate. It's easy to read and slips into the pocket rather neatly. No fuss, no muss.

Now, all we have to do is decide what to put on the flyer. Here's a hint: sex sells. And so does controversy. If your flyer looks kinda boring, nobody will notice. If it's bizarre, people will look at it many times and might even show up to the show in person.

Usually, anything related to sex or controversy is enough to get someone's attention. If you're in a band that is exceptionally good looking, by all means, take advantage of it. You can't be ashamed to use what you were given. If you have an amazing logo, make it prominent on the flyer. You get the picture, right?

Then, we go back to the *less is more* theme—simply list the name of the club, address, day, date, and time of the show. If the person can receive a discount by presenting the flyer at the door, mention that, too. Now, you're done.

If you are a solo artist promoting your own shows, you have no choice but to do everything yourself. But if you're in a four-piece band, split the band into pairs of two, and go your separate ways. It's always easier when there's someone else with you.

Make a list of where people your age hang out—malls, record stores, schools, clubs, movies—and try to hit all of these areas several times before your upcoming show. Introduce yourselves and hand out the flyers. Don't get pissed if someone refuses to take one. Many feel that you're imposing on them and will simply give you the cold shoulder. If that's the case, just move along.

Here's a neat trick if you can pull it off without getting caught: Let's say you're a pop band, and Hanson is playing at your city. Try to sneak into the parking lot and place flyers on the car windshields. If you don't get caught and spend the night in jail (if you do, remember—you didn't read it here), you'll accomplish two important things. One, you'll get to distribute thousands of flyers that will be read. Two, you'll be hitting the exact audience likely to attend your show. Both are crucial to building a following.

Posters

Printing posters (about 11"x17") are a bit more expensive—especially if they're in color, but they make a definite statement and are hard to miss. If you're lucky enough to get an extra hundred bucks or so, do these up in color. Hang them at the club you'll be playing at and also in schools, rehearsal halls, local record stores, etc. Remember to always ask permission to hang posters, and do so in a visible spot. Again, sex and controversy are attention-getters.

Mailing Lists

If you've been sending people around the clubs, collecting names and addresses during your performances, here's where you can benefit. One of the best ways to build a fan base is by calling each and every person on your mailing list a week before your show. If you're shy, don't worry—chances are you will only reach an answering machine anyway. Leave your name, band name, and show information, and invite them to come down and have a good time.

If you have no idea what I'm talking about, just follow these simple directions: During your next show, send a reliable friend through the audience with some paper, pen, and a clipboard. Have her ask each person if they'd mind getting some info in the mail about upcoming shows. Usually, a dozen or so people will volunteer to give you their names, addresses, and telephone numbers to add to your mailing list. Call these people a week before your next show. If you do the same at every show, you'll be surprised at how many names you can accumulate.

It's also a good idea to make friends with other bands in the area so you can all exchange mailing lists and all benefit. However, since the competition is so fierce for drawing power, this is likely to be more of a dream than a reality—but it's worth a shot anyway.

E-Mail

Now that we're all in the computer age, sending someone a flyer or show info via e-mail is a relatively simple thing to do, and, you can actually bulk-mail the notices to dozens of people at the same time. All you need to do is get e-mail addresses when you add names to your mailing list. Or, phone the people and ask if they'll give you their e-mail addresses. Couldn't be more simple.

Flyers, posters, mailing lists, and e-mail are the ways most bands promote their shows and independent CDs. But there are other ways, too, and most of them are FREE!

Calendar Listings

Almost all newspapers, whether the giant dailies or the smaller, independent local papers, have calendar listings for the local clubs. These listings are free. Find out who is in charge of the calendar column, and keep sending in notices at least two weeks in advance. Send your listing along with a photo and your time slot for the particular show. Eventually, when the editor sees your band's name enough times, and you become a staple on the local club scene, you will automatically be listed.

Club Listings

Almost all clubs take out ads in the music sections of the major newspapers on a weekly basis. Call your club booker, and be sure your band is included in those ads. Submit a logo if you have one so your name stands out. Don't take "no" for an answer. It's not gonna cost the club any extra money to include your band's name, and it may help bring a few additional people to the show.

On the purely legal side of things, getting your band's name in ads is a surefire way of owning that name. With regard to keeping a name of a band (assuming nobody already has it), the "use it or lose it" doctrine applies. In other words, you can't just sit at home making up names for bands. You've got to actually go out and use the name in good faith by gigging and promoting it. Bet ya didn't know that!

Press Releases

Although it might be difficult to get one of your self-written press releases into a major newspaper, local papers and magazines can almost always use them. After all, their job is to promote local activities!

Let's start at the beginning. A **press release** is simply information released to the press for them to print. When dealing with the press, there are two important rules to remember:

Rule No. 1:
Never ***send out anything you don't want to see in print.***

Rule No. 2:
There is no such thing as "off the record." **Anything** ***you say, can and will be printed for everyone to read.***

Now that we've discussed what not to do, let's go about the job of finding out how to create one of these press releases.

Press releases should tell the readers *who, what, where, when,* and *how* about a certain artist or activity. You must try to have your press release answer as many of these categories as possible for it to be complete. Here's a short example—see if you get it, OK?

Doud Sets New CD and Tour

Hollywood—Indie recording artist Steven Doud has released his second full-CD, entitled *Come and Get It,* on the Rangerover record label.

Doud, who hails from Pasadena, California, is playing locally (Troubadour, June 12; Key Club, June 16) in support of the release and will announce national tour dates shortly. The artist will be opening his summer tour with three nights in Tempe, Arizona beginning in July.

As the above press release takes the form of an announcement (it can announce *your* record release or your live performance schedule), it answers the questions of "who" (Steven Doud), "what" (CD release and tour dates), and "when" (CD out now, touring in summer, local dates announced in release). "Where" and "how" do not apply in this kind of release.

If you let these five key words serve as your guide to writing press releases, you'll never go wrong—and you'll never fill your releases with extraneous, insignificant fluff, either.

Extraneous, insignificant fluff? Just what do we mean by that? Well, take a look at this:

Beat Boys Play Wine Festival

New York—The Big Apple's most popular rock band, the Beat Boys are at it again, this time announcing a headlining engagement at one of New York's largest outdoor venues, the annual Empire State Wine Festival being held September 4-6 at the Armory on Madison Avenue. The Boys will close the festival and are expected to play before a crowd of over a million people.

Now, let's read this same press release through the eyes of a magazine or newspaper editor:

"Most popular rock band"—Who says so? Can you prove it?

"At it again"—At what? I never heard of this band before.

"Largest outdoor venues"—Central Park is larger. The Armory is indoors.
"Over a million people"—Armory doesn't hold near that many people.

You see what you've done? You've given the editor cause for suspicion. Here's the same press release properly written without the fluff:

Beat Boys Play Wine Festival

New York—New York-based rock band, the Beat Boys, have announced plans to perform at this year's Empire State Wine Festival with a show at the Armory on September 6th, during closing ceremonies.

This single sentence gives the editor all of the necessary information he needs, and leaves him nothing to edit out of your release. So stop trying to hype everything, and just get down to the hard, cold facts. Make it easy on editors. Remember, the less work you make them do, the more likely they are to drop your releases into their columns. And then, everyone wins!

More Homework

Before you even think of sending out a single press release, do your homework! Make a telephone call to the papers or magazines you are about to service with a release, and get the exact spelling of the editor's name and the exact address at which he or she receives mail. Many writers are freelance (meaning they are not on the staff of the paper, but contribute stories to it). These writers sometimes have different mailing addresses. Get them.

Also, don't assume that if an editor's name is John, that he spells it J-O-H-N. It could be spelled J-O-N. Is Sherry spelled "Sherry" or "Sherri"? Is it "Alan," "Allan," or "Allen"? Don't look stupid. Ask and be sure.

Remember what they say about the word "assume." When you assume, you make an "ass" out of "u" and "me"!

It's also very cool to call up a writer and thank him for running your press release. Virtually nobody does that, and I guarantee that you'll take the writer by surprise. Even if you just leave a message on his voice mail you've done a good deed that will help you in the future.

Deadlines and Publication Dates

A **deadline** is a term used by journalists and editors that tells them when a certain story, feature, release, photo, etc. is due. If the deadline for all features at Music Biz magazine is the second Tuesday of each month—no later than 5:00 p.m.—then, if you're writing a feature for that magazine, you know exactly when you need to hand it in.

By getting your press releases into the papers on time you assure that the information in it can be read, edited, and hopefully placed inside. If your story shows up late, it may completely miss the entire issue.

You also need to be aware of the **publication dates** of magazines and newspapers. If you send in a release announcing a show on August 15th, but the magazine doesn't hit the streets until August 23rd, you blew it by not finding out the publication date.

Most national monthly magazines have a three-month lead time which means that stories handed in in April will not hit the newsstands until June or July. This is critical if you're planning a major announcement like tour dates. A simple call to the publication will resolve all doubt. Don't be lazy.

Paid Advertisements

When all else fails, or, in addition to your own promotional campaign, you might want to buy a small paid ad in a local paper or magazine that directly targets your audience.

An ad in the local club section that features your own logo and a club date can cost between $250-$500 depending on the size, popularity of the paper, and the city in which you live. If you have a group of four musicians, that breaks down to between $65-$125 each. You might want to try a small ad for a couple of issues, and see if your attendance grows. If it works, increase the size of the ad. If it doesn't, forget it.

If you decide to gamble with a paid ad, first call the paper or magazine, and ask them to mail you a free schedule of ad rates and ad sizes. This will give you an idea of what you're paying for. It also fills you in on the circulation and age group that the paper appeals to. All of these bits of information are vital in helping you decide whether or not to spend your money.

After you place the ad, always ask your ad representative to send you a copy of the ad *before* it runs. This gives you the opportunity to correct any spelling mistakes or incorrect telephone numbers.

Merchandising

A sure way to earn extra money at gigs and to increase the visibility of your band, or yourself if you're a soloist, is to do some simple merchandising. Lots of times, you automatically get sent merchandising catalogs in the mail, but you throw them away believing them to be junk mail. Now you have a reason to check them out.

If you're not getting them in the mail, check your local yellow pages under merchandising, T-shirts, or novelties, and you'll find plenty of listings.

What you need to keep in mind is that people will only buy certain items of merchandise—those things that are lasting and useful. Refrigerator magnets with your band's logo are nice, but who really cares? On the other hand, beer bottle openers with your logo are useful and can come in quite handy at parties.

Baseball caps and T-shirts are worn all year 'round. Car bumper stickers are inexpensive and travel around from city to city advertising your band! How can you go wrong?

And this brings us to our merchandising checklist. If I said in a previous chapter that there would be no more checklists, I lied! Sorry.

- Be a comparative shopper. Compare prices at different companies before placing any order.
- Find out where the **price breaks** are. The more you order, the less you pay per item. But do not order extra items just to get a lower price!.
- Try to buy several items that you can just give away as a promotion. Matchbooks and bumper stickers with your logos are very inexpensive and would have to be sold at about fifty-cents each. Better to give them away as a show of good faith.
- Logo key chains and bottle openers are also useful and can be sold for a profit at about $2 each.
- If you plan to sell baseball caps and T-shirts, try to do these by mail so you can use the money that comes in to actually buy the merchandise piece-by-piece. Since you always allow 4-6 weeks before shipping out merchandise, this gives the checks plenty of time to clear and time for you to order the goods that were purchased. Pretty sneaky, huh?

Selling your merchandise at live club performances gives you an additional income. But before you set up shop at the venue, ask the club booker if it's OK. Most clubs provide you with a small table and chairs but also take a 20% merchandising fee. So, if you sell $100 worth of merchandise, at the end of the night you need to give $20 to the club.

When setting up at a club, try to tape a giant band poster behind the table so it's visible from across the room. This will make it obvious that you're doing something over at that table. Also, make sure someone is at the merchandise table all night long. You never know when someone is gonna come over to browse.

It's a good idea to bring some extra money with you to make change. Don't assume everyone will have the exact change. And try to sell all the items for even amounts of money—like $5.00, $6.00, $7.50, etc. When you start selling goods for $3.59, you might as well bring a cash register with you to the club.

As a business, you need to keep accurate records of all your sales—large or small—for tax purposes. A simple call to the State Board of Equalization will give you the necessary applications for a **resale number** that lets you charge the *consumer* with paying taxes on the goods that they purchase from you. It's a lot of stupid paperwork, but a necessary evil.

SELF-AWARENESS: The Razor That Slices Between Tragedy and Triumph

by Dennis Anderson

Dennis Anderson

Dennis Anderson is a classically-trained composer and musician with degrees from California State University–Fullerton and the University of Michigan. He is a double Fulbright Scholar and was the 1993 recipient of the Orange County Country Music Association's Audio Engineer of the Year. Anderson was the music editor and recording producer of the feature film Bienvenido Welcome, *which was awarded Mexico's Ariel award for best soundtrack in 1995. He is a freelance engineer and producer. Dennis teaches music courses at Cal State Fullerton, Mt. San Antonio College, and Orange Coast College. He is currently developing a series of digital sonic sculptures to be sold in art galleries and eventually over the Internet. Recently, I had the pleasure of lecturing at one of his classes at Cal State Fullerton. Afterward, as we walked to the cafeteria for lunch, he began telling me these fascinating stories about his life that made some poignant comments on self-promotion and self-awareness. I asked him to please share them with you, and he graciously obliged...*

1. The Fulbright Interview

At the beginning of my last year of graduate studies in music composition at the University of Michigan, the department chairman, Leslie Bassett, asked me if I had ever considered applying for a Fulbright scholarship. I said that I really hadn't because I wasn't sure what that was. "Go over to the Rackham Graduate Studies Hall," he said. "They've got an office and staff that can tell you all about it." I went there and found that a Fulbright scholarship is a way for foreign countries to repay WWII debts to the United States by footing the bill for American students to live there and study. The truth is, I had at least heard of Fulbright scholarships and knew that it involved studying in another country for a year because a girl I had started dating shortly after I moved to Michigan received one and promptly up and left for England. I never heard from her again. But there were some rather interesting composers from England that I thought would be good to study with. Besides that, I wouldn't have to learn another language to go there.

William Albright, the composer with whom I was studying at U of M, suggested Poland in lieu of England because every English-speaking bipedal hominid applied for England, and the most interesting composers of the late twentieth century were in Poland. I had to agree, since Krzysztof Penderecki's work was the most startling and powerful music I had ever heard. His music was used in the film *The Shining,* and his "Threnody for the Victims of Hiroshima" could make the flesh crawl off a stone. Coincidentally, that previous summer I had the opportunity to meet and hang out with the Polish composer/percussionist Marta Ptaszynska who was on an American university circuit tour performing her own compositions.

I asked her what it was like to live in a communist society where the government controlled everybody's lives and regulated the arts. She explained that in Poland, the government not only supported the arts, it actually promoted artists and their careers, and that anybody involved in the arts was on the top of their society. Polish artists, musicians, composers, sculptors, and anyone else involved in creative endeavors were treated with as much respect and admiration as brain surgeons or judges are here in America.

So with Albright's advice to consider Poland, I filled out the fourteen-page application and submitted it. There is an elaborate screening process for a Fulbright grant, and the first weeding-out step is an interview before a panel of educators. My interview was set for October 10th.

At that time, I was composing a piece for harp and percussion. It was a challenging piece at the virtuoso level. I had taken it upon myself to actually take harp lessons to learn the instrument well enough to write for it, and I wanted to bring it along with me to the Fulbright interview, where the committee would be examining examples of my work. I was frantically trying to finish copying the piece so it would be ready. I worked day and night for the last three days before my interview. As the interview time approached, I realized that not only was I not going to be able to clean myself up, I wasn't even going to have time to change out of the sweater I had been wearing for the last three days and nights. I had seen other students waiting for their interview dressed in suits and ties. It goes without saying that I was mentally obliterated, and all hope was lost. I had seen an interview with Canadian singer Leon Redbone where he answered every question with a wry chuckle and decided that I might as well just show up in this smelly sweater and sunglasses and gaze out the window, chuckling at their questions.

I finished the ink copy of my harp-and-percussion piece with exactly enough time to run into a Kinko's and make one copy to bring along to the interview. To make matters worse, I went to the wrong building on the other side of Ann Arbor, and that caused me to be forty-five minutes late for my interview. When I arrived, the committee was leaving but granted me the interview anyway. I was so tired and charged with adrenaline that I went into a state of mind that was actually sublime—thinking that there was no way on earth they were going to take me seriously.

Lesson: The amazing fact is that they were so impressed with my casual, highly-focused attitude that they recommended me for the grant. Because I hadn't had time to sit and fester into a state of intellectual "goo" as all other applicants are known to do, I came across as exactly the kind of person they wanted to represent the United States. The truth of the matter was, I wasn't trying to be anybody but myself—take it or leave it. That was the deciding factor in their assessment of me as a Fulbright applicant.

The following September, I arrived in Warsaw to begin my stay in Poland as a Fulbright Scholar. I was given a second Fulbright scholarship the following year.

2. Less Than Best

Comedienne Minnie Pearl often gave symposiums for young performers entering the entertainment industry. During these lectures, she would relate a story that happened to her during her early years as a touring comic:

In 1943, Minne was on the road making the best of whatever situation she found herself in, as so many fledgling entertainers often do. On one stop in a remote rural town somewhere in the Midwest, she noticed that the audience was dismally sparse and largely unresponsive to her performance. Not feeling particularly inspired, she went through the motions and gave what even she herself felt was a lackluster performance. When she finished her routine, her manager met her backstage. He furiously scolded her for turning in a mediocre performance. Minnie told him that she didn't see how it could matter all that much.

True, the crowd had been small and basically unresponsive to her act. This time though, it really did matter because one of the people in the audience had come all the way from New York just to see her, and had been trying to catch up with her for weeks. This particular show was the only opportunity he had to see her. It seems he had just written a musical and had her in mind for the part of Aido Annie in his Broadway musical *Oklahoma!* Of course, having seen a performance that was at best indifferent, Richard Rodgers went back to New York to continue looking for the right person to cast for the part. The tragic irony of it all was that Minnie Pearl had always aspired to become a Broadway actress, and had she performed her routine at the level that is now legendary, she might have had an entirely different life.

Lesson: At her lectures for young entertainers, Minnie always caps this story with the advice that one should never step out on a stage and give less than their absolute best. You never know who is in the audience!

3. The One That Got Away

While working as a freelance engineer in Nashville, I was often called to produce singer-songwriter demos at Music Row Productions, a sixteen-track studio that marketed itself by placing pamphlets on the registration desk of various motels in the Music Row vicinity. Needless to say, the clientele were usually less than professional. I often referred to these sessions as the "singing-impaired" demo sessions: people who were totally devoid of any musical ability, but who had scraped enough cash together to catch a greyhound to Nashville, would try to make a few demo recordings so they could get signed to a major record label and become stars. An example of what I'm talking about would be the response one client made to my request to try doing a count-off before starting to play: "I'm not real sure about the difference between beats and chords," he said. With that, I leaned into the talkback mic and soothingly said, "You know, it doesn't really matter. Why don't you just play, and I'll record it!"

I sometimes found myself at the console, exasperated, with head in hands, consoling myself with the notion that Jimmy Bowen and Jerry Crutchfield must have had to go through this kind of experience before they worked their way up to producing national recording artists.

After one particularly grueling morning of these projects, a fellow named John came in to record some guitar-vocal demos. I was relieved to hear him actually tune his guitar as he prepared to sing his songs. As he began the first of three songs, I was astonished to hear a truly wonderful voice, singing with heartfelt conviction. The three-song session was over in about four takes. I told him that he was a great singer with a lot of potential, and I would love to help him get a record deal and produce him. He seemed genuinely grateful that I would want to help him. He gave me the phone number of the girlfriend he lived with in Kentucky, and we agreed to get back in touch the following week. He left a cassette copy of the three songs we had recorded, and he headed back to Kentucky.

I phoned up Jerry Teifer, vice president at Acuff Rose Music. Jerry was the first person in the industry I had met after moving to Nashville, and he had taken a liking to me. Our first meeting closed with his offer to help me in any way he could. I figured this was the time to call in that offer. I told him I had found someone that had real artist potential and asked him if he could help me find a record label for this guy. I told him I had a guitar-vocal cassette demo, and Jerry said to come over and play it for him. After one listen through the first song, Jerry suggested that John and I both come to his office the following Tuesday so he could meet John. I set up a lunch meeting with John for that Tuesday before our meeting with Jerry. John arrived dressed in full country regalia, looking like a million bucks. We had lunch and drove over to Jerry's office. John brought his guitar.

We walked into Jerry's office and sat on the couch. He asked John to play something for him, and John obliged. Jerry agreed that John had what it took and should have a major label deal. This was the Jerry Teifer who had picked up a phone and made one call to land Kathy Mattea her first record deal, and I knew that if he thought this singer could make it that there would be a deal at the end of our endeavors, with me as the producer of a major label artist.

"What we need to do now," he explained, "is to round up some money to get this all under way. I'll start making some calls." He told me to keep in touch. "Do you think he's serious?" John asked as we left the building. I told him about Kathy Mattea and told him to keep in close contact with me.

A few days later, I talked to Jerry Teifer, and he said he hadn't come up with anything yet but that he was waiting to hear back from some people. I called the number John had given me and was told that he and his girlfriend had had a falling out and that he had moved out, leaving no forwarding number. After a couple of weeks, I got a call from John. "Jerry Kennedy wants to produce me," he said. "What do you think I ought to do?" "Well," I said, "I don't have the reputation Kennedy has. I guess you should do what you think is right." I had that sinking feeling one gets as the oceanliner you just fell off of begins to disappear over the horizon.

I called Jerry Teifer and told him that John had been approached by Jerry Kennedy, and I didn't figure I was going to be involved with him any longer. Teifer reminded me that Kennedy had a lot of pull in the industry, and it looked like this fish had gotten away.

Five years later, when I was working as a house engineer at the Crazy Horse nightclub in California, I saw a promotional CD in the DJ's booth. It was the forthcoming album of a new artist by the name of John Michael Montgomery. It was not produced by Jerry Kennedy. In fact, the producer was someone I had never heard of.

Lesson: The reason that I was not that producer was that I had been honest and humble in an industry that does not use those two words in the same sentence. I had forgotten who I was and what my qualifications really were. I was a double Fulbright scholar! I held a Masters degree in music from one of the top four universities in the country. I had crashed the back-stage entrance of the Grand Ole Opry every Friday and Saturday night for eight months just to observe and learn everything I could about how country music was put together. Most importantly, I had one of the most powerful men in Nashville going to bat for me. I forgot that I was every bit as capable of producing a national artist as Jimmy Bowen or Jerry Kennedy. George Martin had never produced a rock band before he took on the Beatles! While there's nothing wrong with being honest, it is absolutely imperative that one has the courage to believe in oneself.

4. Doing the Impossible

In 1989, I submitted an application to Opryland for a live sound mixing job. I had up to that time only engineered in recording studios, but I figured I could handle their music revue shows. In the summer, I got a call from their sound department to interview for a position. They told me that there was a position that had opened up on the General Jackson Showboat and was in immediate need of filling. Apparently, I was being offered the position because I had indicated on my resume that I had mixed a live recording of a Maynard Fergusen concert for a cable TV station, and Maynard was the sound department manager's favorite artist. That was all they needed to know, and I accepted the position.

I came in mid-season, so the show had already been running seven nights a week for several months. There was a member of the sound department riding for the first month to "show me the ropes" on this 300-foot paddlewheeler. The room where the main show took place was 100' by 40' and was a steel-and-glass room floating in water—a totally impossible situation for live sound. So much so that my predecessor had literally cracked and marched into the general manager's office one day and chewed him to bits, which got him fired from the position before he had made it out of the manager's office door.

I had to develop my own system for doing everything with the goal of making my job run as smoothly as possible, so I employed every trick I could to get the show sounding like a record since that was what I was used to doing in studios. I was very successful at getting the best sound they had ever had on the boat, according to Don Martin, the show's producer. Eventually, the head of the sound department took me aside and asked me how I did it. I told him the audio tricks I was using to eliminate feedback and bring vocals and instruments into the pocket as they sure needed. He said that everything I was doing was at best unconventional, but to keep doing it since the results were so good. He said that everyone before me had tried to run the sound "by the book" and had run screaming.

Lesson: I was able to succeed where others had failed because I didn't know that it was impossible. I had to think on my feet and do the best I could, and that was what the task required.

5. Best Soundtrack

In January of 1994, a few days after the Northridge earthquake, I got a phone call from a guy who was in desperate need of someone to help him create a film score using MIDI instead of a live orchestra. The film was a feature-length production from Mexico. Apparently, there was no budget for an orchestra, and this composer, who introduced himself as Angel Romero, was saddled with the task of somehow pulling off the music end of the project. He was so forlorn and worried about it that I immediately wanted to help him.

I had been recommended by some long chain of referrals, and I had to confess to him that I didn't know who he was. He explained that he was Angel RRRRRRRomerrrrrrro—the classical guitarist. I apologized for not being familiar with his work because, for the past several years, I had been deeply involved in the commercial country music world. He was genuinely amused that I didn't know who he was. He cheerfully explained that we could work together because of that very fact. "Too many people that I try to work with are in too much awe of me, and I hate that," he explained. He reiterated that time was running out, and there was virtually no budget to work with. "Look," I said, "let's worry about the money later and get this work done. That's what is most important at this moment." "I'm coming immediately," he exclaimed. "I live in Del Mar, about an hour from you, but I will fly up and be there as soon as I can get there." He arrived at my door about three hours later.

The film, *Bienvenido Welcome,* was a delight of a project. The plot and script were astounding. It had all the makings of a film collaboration between Woody Allen and Federico Fellini. When it became clear that Angel was going to have to drive daily up to my apartment where I had my studio set up in my bedroom, he became extremely anxious and convinced me that I should break it down and move it into his mansion in Del Mar, where I would be able to work with him around the clock. He explained that his friends Bill Conti and Bruce Broughton do this, and that they have "gurus" who make the whole thing work, and that was what he needed. I was to be his production/arrangement/recording guru. That worked for me. Besides, I really liked this guy. He had a great sense of humor and played his ass off. Not only that, he was a Spanish Knight! Andre Segovia was his teacher and mentor, and he claimed to have taught the Beach Boys the little ostinato at the beginning of "Sloop John B" while helping them work out the contrapuntal vocal arrangements in a New York hotel room. Angel and I became fast friends immediately.

This project entailed Angel sketching out some musical ideas on $8^1/_2$ x11 manuscript paper and me arranging it on my little Macintosh Classic computer equipped with nothing more than Mark of the Unicorn's Performer 4.2, combined with a Roland SC55 Sound Canvas, a Korg M1, and one (that's *one*) Sony video recorder. I didn't have the heart to tell Angel that I had no synchronization capability. I had scored student films back at the University of Michigan, and I figured things would work out OK. By timing out each cue and literally "punching" each hit point in real time as the video worktape rolled, I was able to set the music to the scenes manually. We didn't need no stinkin' synchronization! I worked day and night in Angel's house in Rancho Santa Fe using this highly non-technical approach.

With regard to the actual working environment, there was a lot to be desired. He informed me as we approached his neighborhood that he and his fiancé lived, in his words, "a somewhat Bohemian lifestyle"—largely due to the fact that he was on tour most of the time. He had bought this ranch a few months earlier and had begun renovating it, but the work was in progress at the time. "In progress" actually meant that there were no external walls in some places—just sheets of colored Plexiglas to keep coyotes out. There were no shingles on the roof so one could actually look through the cracks between the ceiling boards into the beautiful star-filled night sky. This became a problem when the worst storm season since the 1992 El Niño rolled in a few days after I moved in there. I had to work while streams of water were pouring in through the cracks in the ceiling. That meant moving the whole studio from room to room as the flooding washed me out of each location like a troublesome gopher. We finally went down to a hardware store and bought plastic dropcloth to string up across the room to create a sort of tent that caused the rainwater to drain off overhead into a bucket in the corner of the room.

In spite of all the adversity, work progressed well, and when Gabriel Retes, the director, came up from Mexico City to see the final version of the score, he actually went out in the driveway and cried, telling Angel he was completely overwhelmed by the music. Over dinner that night in Del Mar, Retes told us that his absolute favorite part of the score was a particularly powerful scene where the main actor walks into the bathroom of the hotel where he has just had an affair with a woman he had met the night before and sees the words "Welcome to the world of AIDS" scrawled in lipstick on the mirror. I nearly fell out of my chair when Angel quickly said, "Dennis wrote that cue." It's well-known in inner circles of the film music world that the "gurus" often are given the task of actually creating cues themselves. That sort of thing goes with the territory, and in the real world of film scoring, these arranger/orchestrater/engineer/etceteras are paid well enough to be happy in their work. But I would never have felt that Angel shouldn't have the credit for my work, and I told him so when we had a moment together later that evening. "What do you mean?" he exclaimed. "I'm not that low of a person to take credit for something you did." Angel's quick reply to that situation demonstrated firsthand why he is deserving of the title of Spanish Knight.

Lesson: The film was met with an enthusiastic response at its premiere in Mexico. In 1995, it was awarded Mexico's Ariel award for best soundtrack, their version of the American Oscar. This all came to pass because I was not intimidated by the fact that I did not have the necessary technology to produce and synchronize the score, and it didn't matter to me that he was one of the greatest living musicians, nor was I intimidated by his stature as a decorated person of great importance. What was important at the time was that the work needed to be completed and I couldn't let Angel down. I gave it everything I had and flew by the seat of my pants to get the results that were needed. When all is said and done, it's the results that count—not the methods used to achieved them.

11 Meeting & Greeting

Ever get tired of people in this business telling you that it's "who you know" that can make the difference between success and failure? Me too! So why don't you do something about it? Oh—I'm supposed to *tell* you what to do, right? OK. Find people who can help move your career forward. There, that was easy enough for me. Was it good for you, too?

Networking, schmoozing, pressing the flesh, meeting and greeting—it's all the same. It's all about getting out there and mingling with people in the industry. Easy to say, difficult to do. Consider this: there are literally hundreds of parties, celebrations, conventions, galas, and get-togethers in the music industry every year. And you will not be invited to attend a single one of them. Not very comforting, but true, nonetheless.

The "In Crowd"

The best way to become part of the "in crowd" is to hang in their circles. But you can only do that if you're part of the business, itself. No problem. Become part of the business! Oh—you want some more help, I see. How about this: Become an **intern.** Yeah, you heard me, an intern. There are always record companies, publishing companies, management offices, and recording studios looking for free help. *That means you!*

There is no better way to learn about the inner workings of the music business than to be a part of the inner workings. As an intern, you will get valuable hands-on experience, and at the same time, you'll be meeting, greeting, and mingling with others already inside the biz. Some internships actually pay, but don't hold your breath. It's the experience you want and not the few dollars they'll throw at you.

Once you get an internship, very casually feel your way around the office. Find out who's who. Ask questions without making a nuisance of yourself. Do your job well so you are trusted and given more responsibilities. You'd be surprised at how far you can get with a good personality and some hard work. Keep your eyes and ears open—listen for inter-office gossip, and be ready to strike!

After interning for two to three months, you'll be a trusted member of the company and privy to party invites and light socializing. You might get invited to a record release party or a movie screening. *Go to all of them,* even if they seem boring to you. Fact is, you never know what other important people will attend. Truth is, considering your status in the business, almost anyone else you meet should be regarded as important! Don't be lazy. Having you nails done is not a good enough reason to miss an industry event.

Always carry several copies of your demo tape with you. Keep extras in your car, but always put at least two or three in you jacket or pants pockets. After all, that's why you're at the event, isn't it?

Be selective and plan your moves. Don't walk around the room handing out demos as if they were finger sandwiches. Be careful, or someone will take a bite out of you. Do not be obvious. Sometimes, it's best to wait until you're asked. Other times, it's OK to lead the person into asking you for a demo tape. Always remember that someone else was kind enough to invite you to this function and that you'll want more invites. So don't ruin it by being too pretentious or aggressive. There will be other days.

Another good way to meet and greet is to attend seminars, talks, conventions, and workshops where industry speakers and big-wigs gather to impart their knowledge to the less fortunate. That's *you*! Some of these events are free, others may cost. If you are interning at a music business company, you might be invited to attend for free or at least be entitled to a professional industry discount.

Pick your spots—especially if you're paying full price for admission. At what event can I meet the people who will do me the most good? Where am I most likely to hand out my tapes? Where will I gain the most knowledge?

If you're attending a convention, be sure to make your way around to every single booth to "taste" the varied fruits of music business information. Many conventions have multiple themes and many important guest speakers. In most cases, dozens of topics relevant to those in the business are discussed in panel Q&A formats. These are great because each panel usually boasts five or six top industry figures. After the panel, make the rounds, dude. Go over and congratulate the speakers on a job well done. Tell them how much you've learned from their suggestions. Tell them how valuable their advice was. Befriend them! And then, very subtly, ask if they'll accept one of your demo tapes, which you just so happen to be carrying with you.

If, for some reason, you just can't find the time to intern, check out the "calendar" or "bulletin board" columns in your local music papers and magazines for upcoming events that you can attend. Every city in America has them at one time or another. You may have to attend a lecture or seminar that is completely unrelated to your field of interest just to meet someone of importance. *Do it.*

Another good idea is to try to get a job in a place that record people frequent—record stores, tape duplication places, rock clubs. Get the idea? Then all you need to do is your job, and hopefully, every now and again, someone important will walk in, and you pull out a tape from your back pocket. A good friend of mine, J.T. Harding, got signed to EMI years ago by giving the label's vice president, Brian Koppelman, a demo tape. You see, J.T. worked at Tower Records/Sunset and always carried his tapes to work with him. I told you it works!

What to Say

The people within the music industry are just like you—they all eat and sleep and go to the toilet. They buy clothes and groceries and go to the movies. So when you run into them, be yourself. Be natural. But above all else, know what you want to say. Here's what not to say when, for example, you meet your guitar idol:

> "Wow! I can't believe it's really you. You're my idol, dude. Man, this is awesome! You blow me away, dude. Can I have your autograph?"

On the other hand, a conversation like this is more orderly, educational, and compelling. And, likely to impress the artist:

> "Hey, nice to meet you, man. I love your album. The guitar sound in 'Killing Man' was awesome—how'd ya get it? [Wait for answer] Cool. mind if I have your autograph? Thanks a lot."

See the difference? This second conversation is real. You're letting him know you liked his record and found something special about it that you want him to explain. That makes *him* feel important. By taking this approach, you're talking with the artist on artistic terms—terms he understands best. You're not acting like a groupie out for a quick autograph. After that, of course he'll give you his autograph!

Telephone Talk

The very same is true for making telephone calls to executives. Sound certain. Sound like the voice of authority. Sound focused. But sound pleasant.

> "Hello, Kenny Kerner calling for Bill, please."
> "May I tell him what this is regarding?"
> "I'm returning his call. It's regarding my band, Cartoon Boyfriend."

Everything is straight to the point. No room for misunderstandings. Notice I mentioned that I was returning his call. That tells the assistant that *he* called *me* first, and that he is *expecting* me to call back!

Be aware of the fact that on the phone, certain letters sound alike and need to be spelled out. For example, it's often hard to distinguish a "D" from a "G" or "E." An "F" and an "S" also sound alike over the phone. So take that extra few seconds to spell your name out or get the exact spelling of the person you're calling.

Looks Can Kill

Remember that people often form an opinion of you by the way you look and stand. Nobody said it was right, but it happens all the time. If you see a messy-looking girl with a pretty smile and a disheveled appearance, chances are you won't be around long enough to find out about her personality or her education. Your brain tells you to *pass* on this one. And you do.

Getting dressed to the max isn't the answer, either. Just look presentable and stand tall—show your conviction in your question or your response to a question. Remember that your body language is always talking even though you may not be. The person who once said that you don't get a second chance to make a first impression was right on the money!

Getting Ahead

Ever notice that even if you dial an executive's direct office number you'll always get his or her assistant? Does that give you any clues? Like maybe the one way to get to the top man is through the bottom man? Like maybe if the assistant becomes your friend, you'll be able to open doors once closed?

Ever wonder how much these assistants make? Very little. Ever wonder how much respect these assistants get? Very little. Ever wonder how much music business knowledge they have? Very little. Ever wonder how much power they have? *Lots!*

Because they can put your call through or just pretend to be taking a message, and you won't be the wiser.

So why not make them feel more important than they really are? Why not befriend them in the hopes of them helping you in the future? Why not ask if you can send them your tapes for some input? Why not ask their opinion?

Heard this advice before? Well then, take it. There's no better way of getting "inside" than through someone already on the "inside." If our assistant loves your tape, it makes him/her look and feel like a hero. If they find the tape disappointing, they feel obliged to pass it to their boss for a final comment. And, you've made a friend at the label regardless of what happens. Can you say "win-win"?

Knowing how to network is a major part of getting ahead in the music business. Knowing how to be creative is even more important. Combining the two is the answer.

PEOPLE POWER

by Dan Kimpel

Dan Kimpel

Dan Kimpel is a Los Angeles-based personal manager and PR consultant. He is the author of Networking in the Music Business *(Writer's Digest Books) and the editor of Film Music Magazine. He also writes and edits "Songworks" for Music Connection magazine and "Songbook" for Grammy Magazine. His recent credits as a concert/event producer include Quincy Jones, Joni Mitchell, Randy Newman, John Fogerty, Glen Ballard, and Ashford & Simpson. Kimpel is an amazingly confident public speaker and an acknowledged expert on schmoozing—or "networking" as he likes to call it. Pay close attention to what he has to say because this is the real deal! Take it away, Dan!*

"Who you know, what you know, who knows you," is the mantra I first evolved in my book, *Networking in the Music Business*. Since its publication, I've enjoyed the open doors of authorhood: wonderful opportunities to travel the world, to speak at colleges, universities, and conferences, and to meet readers whose own expectations and ambitions have been fueled by my words. As rewarding as these experiences have been, however, they have also led me to one harsh realization:

The people who really need this information will never get it.

Why? Because many aspirants in the music business would rather fumble their way into oblivion with insecurity and self-defeat mechanisms intact. Rather than learn what the business is —and how to integrate themselves into it—many prefer to wander the darkness without lighting the lantern of knowledge, dependent instead upon hearsay, opinion, and attitude. Many would rather be told what to do than figure out their own options.

Here's a statement of truth, my friends: In my thirty-three years in the music business, every deal I've ever seen go down is a direct result of a personal contact. If you send your tapes, CDs, and press kits into the oblivious void of unsolicited material, you will reap what you sow; nothing. If you rely on the overhyped, overpriced expertise of so called "experts," you are simply adding to their profit margin, while doing nothing for yourself.

"But there are companies that will put my music on the Internet," you say. Well, I ask you, does this lead to a personal contact? "But," you go on, "I can pay $XXXX per year to have my songs sent to record and publishing companies." Again, does this lead to a personal contact?

It is not always possible to predict career paths. But many times, success is determined by the act of putting yourself in a position where things can happen.

People respond to others who are open, honest, and sincere. Many of the rules of good etiquette apply just as strongly in the music business as they do in other areas of social interaction. (Just because someone has blue hair and a pierced cheek doesn't mean they are hostile or alienated; this is show business.) As in every other business on the planet, people like to do business with their friends. To make an impact in the music world, you have to be in the loop, and this takes time. When I first journeyed to Los Angeles in the early eighties, I made it my business to meet as many people as possible. Today, almost twenty years later, I find that the struggling songwriters, starving musicians, and hustling promoters are now the platinum songwriters, triple-scale session cats, and record company vice presidents of today. True, many left the business, unable to take the pressures and rejection. You can never win a game if you get up from the table. For those who stayed, endured, evolved, and reinvented themselves, their careers flourished.

"I was out of it, now I'm getting back into it," is a statement I often hear from musicians and artists desiring to return to music. But the music business is not a canoe. One can't leap onto shore, set up camp, and then expect to leap back in the boat. If you attempt this, you'll find that the current has carried your transportation far downstream. And as a result, you're all wet. The commitment to your career can't be constrained by false time lines. You really can't have anything else to fall back on other than your own ingenuity, resourcefulness, and, most essentially, your network.

I recently signed an act I manage to a major record deal. I first met him when he volunteered in my office at the Los Angeles Songwriters Showcase, now a part of the National Academy of Songwriters. I became involved in his career when I booked him to perform at an outdoor festival in Los Angeles. From my backstage vantage point, I could observe that he won audiences over rhythmically, melodically, and by a judicious use of eye contact to connect everyone within his visual range.

Over the next four years I observed, and channeled, his artistic growth. He was utterly committed to his music; he presented himself as someone with no other options. Eventually, through a combination of contacts, chance, and timing, a record company noticed him, too.

I would like to share with you the reasons he was signable:

1. He's sold 10,000 CDs on his own.
2. He performs an average of eighteen shows a month, every month.
3. He isn't dependent upon trends, fashion, or being "this year's model."
4. His music (Latin/World) appeals to a wide, upscale demographic.
5. He can easily cross over from a niche market into the mainstream.

6. He is young enough to have a long career in the music business.
7. He has a vivid artistic vision.
8. Audiences respond to him.
9. He is secure in his art; he knows exactly what he wants.
10. He would be doing his music even without his deal.

If something doesn't happen naturally or easily, many times it may never happen at all. This is not an excuse to slack off, or not do your work, but music is very grass-roots oriented and possesses a natural flow of measured enthusiasm. My client's audiences grew continuously from his first shows. We never had to beg or harangue people to come see him perform; they wanted to.

In the latter half of this decade, we can observe that record company signings are a result of street buzz. In the old days, massive billboards and hype campaigns were marketing tools. Today, overhype can spell disaster. The methods are much more subtle. For bands and artists just beginning their careers, local support is essential to global viability.

I observe that opportunities for musicians, songwriters, producers, and marketing people are much wider now than at any point in past history. New forms of music— many based on new technologies—give unprecedented opportunities for growth. As creative people, we need to be aware of lateral growth as well as vertical. Creative people need challenges and changes to help them achieve fulfillment. For songwriters, the obvious growth markets are film, television, video, and new media.

But as the technology becomes more prevalent, good people skills become even crucial. Creativity suffers in isolation, and music is a cooperative venture. Your success will ultimately be determined by being the kind of person others wish to see, and can help, succeed.

Rewind: Looking Back

I must have started this chapter a dozen times and then changed my mind. Why the hell would anyone want to know about my life in the music business? Who really cares, anyway? Then it dawned on me that almost every single word in this book is based on an experience that I actually lived. I realized that, like you, I'm taking this ride alone. I'm flying without a net. Thirty years and counting.

The more I thought about trashing it, the more vital it seemed. What better way of educating you than to stand before you naked, saying "Here—this is my life in the music business. Here's how I messed up. Here's how I was screwed. Here's how I succeeded. Here's what I learned. Here's how I managed to have a career that's lasted some thirty years." All of a sudden, this chapter seemed very important. Crucial. And so I began again.

From Whence I Came

Take #13: I was born in 1947 and lived, for many years, on the lower east side of Manhattan—311 East Third Street, to be exact. I have one brother, Barry, who is a doctor, and a sister, Joyce, who is a social worker. Nobody in my family is in any way even remotely connected to the music business.

My parents worked incredibly hard, sometimes two jobs a day, to make life easy for us. They gave us everything we ever needed: love, shelter, food, clothing, toys—you name it. All they ever asked was that we each stay out of trouble and get a good education so we'd have a career when we were adults.

My only connection to music as a kid was listening to my parents' giant Webcor phonograph player that they kept in the living room of our apartment. It played 78s, and we had dozens of them. I vaguely remember some titles like "The Naughty Lady of Shady Lane" and "Come On-A My House" and a few Elvis singles, too. Sometimes I'd pick up the throw pillow that was on the couch and use it as a pretend guitar and mimic the Elvis records in front of the living room mirror. But that was it.

One Saturday afternoon, my mother took me and my brother for a walk. We strolled a few miles from the house and found ourselves on 14th Street amidst dozens of bargain stores selling cameras, radios, stereo equipment, wallets, lamps, and just about anything they could get their hands on. A few minutes later, we both walked out of a store with radios—his was black, mine red.

The Little Red Box

I couldn't wait to get home and check it out. Now, I could play music whenever I wanted and not have to ask permission to use the phonograph.

I got home and immediately placed the radio squarely on the ledge of the window that jutted out into my bedroom. I kneeled down in front of it and turned it on. My life was about to change forever.

I slowly turned the dial until I heard some popular music that I was familiar with. I stopped at WMGM—a Top 40 radio station that played the popular (pop) music of the time and also broadcast Martin Block's "Make Believe Ballroom" countdown show on Saturday mornings. Though I had no idea at the time, listening to that weekly show gave me my first real experience at picking hit records.

Each Saturday morning, the program would play the Top 40 most popular singles in the country. Along with the survey, they'd debut new records just released and mention those debuting on the chart for the first time. After a few weeks time, I began to make a list of the new songs I felt would hit the charts. My accuracy was astonishing. I seemed to have had an inborn talent for knowing and feeling what elements went into the making of a chart single—and all at the age of about nine or ten.

Listening to the radio for hours a day also acquainted me with the many different styles of music in the fifties. In those days, there was no separation of genres—no pop and R&B and metal and country. It was just plain music. All kinds of music—good music.

For example, the singles that reached #1 during 1955 were:

"Let Me Go Lover"	Joan Weber (pop/female)
"Hearts of Stone"	The Fontaine Sisters (pop/female group)
"Sincerely"	The McGuire Sisters (pop/female group)
"The Ballad of Davy Crockett"	Bill Hayes (pop/male—TV & movie hero)
"Cherry Pink and Apple Blossom White"	Perez Prado (pop/instrumental)
"Dance With Me Henry"	Georgia Gibbs (pop/female)
"Unchained Melody"	Les Baxter (pop/instrumental from film)
"Rock Around the Clock"	Bill Haley & The Comets (rock 'n' roll/group)
"Learnin' the Blues"	Frank Sinatra (pop/male)
"The Yellow Rose of Texas"	Mitch Miller (pop/sing-a-long)
"Ain't That a Shame"	Fats Domino (rock 'n' roll/male)
"Love Is a Many-Splendored Thing"	The Four Aces (pop/group)
"Autumn Leaves"	Roger Williams (pop/instrumental)
"Sixteen Tons"	Tennessee Ernie Ford (pop/male)

I began to notice the mixture of styles and sounds on the charts: country, instrumental, male and female vocalists, movie themes, groups, big bands, rock 'n' roll. I began to focus in on the sounds of the records, the vocal qualities of the lead singers. I was able to tell a record by Frank Sinatra or Perry Como or Connie Francis or the Four Seasons after only a single note or two.

Suddenly, listening to the radio became fascinating. There was a new depth to what I was doing. Without knowing, I began to scrutinize the records and analyze their individual sounds. I was able to tell one artist from the next instantly. Little did I know at the time, that I was actually building the basis of my career in the music business.

Today, most A&R guys are lacking a deeply-rooted knowledge and appreciation of music. Their appreciation goes all the way back to Nirvana and then stops. In the fifties, records like "El Paso," "On the Wings of a Dove," "Wolverton Mountain," and "He'll Have to Go" were pop records. Today, they're called country and are only played on "oldies" radio stations. How many A&R guys know that the Beatles' record of "Till There Was You" was a song from *The Music Man* and not a Lennon-McCartney tune? I learned all of this stuff by listening to the radio. By listening to every kind of music possible.

The Beat Goes On

Like most kids, as I grew older, I got more and more into music. By the time I was a sophomore in high school, my family and I had moved to Brooklyn—a couple blocks away from Prospect Park, right off Flatbush Avenue. I was already singing in and managing a band and loving every minute of it. But still, the thought of actually having a career that dealt with music was nonexistent. We played for the fun of it. It never got deeper than that.

In 1964, when the Beatles posted an amazing nineteen hit singles on the charts, I had just turned seventeen. Their enormously-successful invasion of America didn't overwhelm me as much as the campaign mounted by Capitol Records to merchandise the British band. I was already familiar with hit records, but the Beatles' bobbing-heads, point-of-purchase, in-store display to sell "I Want to Hold Your Hand" was new to me.

Until this point in time, I believed that people heard records on the radio, went into their local record store and bought them. I never dreamed that it was also possible to advertise those records inside the stores themselves. What a cool idea, I thought. Someone just walking into the store to look around might actually be persuaded to buy a Beatles record after seeing all of the great in-store merchandising and advertising items. (I used this advertising tie-in later on to promote local shows with a three-piece rock band called Dust that I managed and wrote songs for.)

My record collection had grown to a few hundred albums. I attended Erasmus Hall High School which was located just across the street from Halperin's, a local record store that became my afterschool headquarters. Day in, day out, you'd find me browsing through the new releases that were just delivered to the store. It never dawned on me that all of the artists there actually had to be signed by a record company executive. All I knew was that once a week, a truck stopped in front of the store and dropped off a selection of new music for me to hear.

The diverse tastes in music that I developed as a child stayed with me through my teens and into my twenties. As a result, I had a pretty eclectic collection of records, with LPs by Ars Nova, Ultimate Spinach, Clear Light, and a British quintet called Dave Dee, Dozy, Beaky, Mick & Tich, to name just a few. Weekends would find me in Greenwich Village checking out the new rock bands.

Going Pro, Almost

By the late sixties, something new called FM radio was now in vogue, and music was all around me. I was now attending Hunter College in Manhattan and really hating it. I couldn't find anything to hold my interest, save for an English Literature class taught by a Professor Albert. I knew I wasn't long for the education system the day I joined the college newspaper, the Hunter Envoy. But sometimes, a black cloud has a silver lining. This one did.

While working on the newspaper, I befriended another student named Stan Fein, who worked in some kind of student activities program and was responsible for bringing concerts to the college. Fein worked with a then new local promoter named Ron Delsener (now the top promoter in New York for the last several decades).

I used my position at the college newspaper to solicit interviews with famous rock stars and to get into concerts for free. One of the first publicists I encountered was a pretty, British woman named Nancy Lewis who represented a wild rock quartet called The Who. I remember meeting Nancy at the Gorham Hotel one afternoon. For years, the Gorham had the reputation of being New York's #1 "rock star" hotel.

Nancy gave me a copy of the British version of The Who's latest album, and we walked in to meet Roger Daltry and Pete Townshend. That was the beginning of my career as a real rock journalist. On the way home, I don't think my feet touched the ground once. It wasn't that I was in awe of meeting them but that I had done a real, credible interview with a famous band. For the first time, I had done something professional.

I was fascinated by the history of these bands—how they got together, how they struggled, how they overcame adversity. It struck me that they encountered the very same problems we did with our local bands. And so I continued to learn. I continued to store pertinent information in my brain, subject to recall at a later date.

My next major interview found me at the Gorham again, this time talking with Eric Clapton and Jack Bruce of Cream. I can't remember what we spoke about during the separate interviews. I only remember that Eric tried playing his guitar with his toes in an attempt (a joke, of course) to out-do Hendrix, and Jack taught me how to snort cocaine through the barrel of a cheap ballpoint pen—a trick that came in handy later in life. Eric and I got on famously. So much so that he decided to take me to see Bob Dylan's movie *Don't Look Back* instead of performing at Stonybrook University that night. My brother, who was attending the college, was pissed because, at my insistence, he had bought tickets to the show.

All during this time, Ron Delsener continued to present concerts at Hunter College, and I continued to suggest artists to perform. The first big show I remember at Hunter featured the Doors. Writing the music column for the paper also meant that I got to hang out backstage for the entire show, and this made me privy to all of the gossip, rumors, and group arguments—more stuff for me to learn and file away. I never got off on actually *meeting* the rock stars, but rather on the information I was able to pry out of them and use later in life. This particular night, everyone was on edge because concert time was fast approaching and, as usual, there was no sign of singer Jim Morrison. The remaining three band members paced furiously backstage, cursing him with their every breath—but still no Jimbo.

My head started throbbing, so I decided to walk out the stage entrance door and get some much-needed fresh air. As I began to stretch and breathe in the cool night air, a taxi cab roared down the street, coming to a dead halt in front of the stage door. "Is this Hunter College?" the driver asked, with a quizzical look on his face. "Yeah," I replied, as I walked into the gutter and flung open the back door of the cab to find a leather-clad Jim Morrison slumped across the back seat. The starry-eyed singer looked up at me and asked, "What city are we in?" Right then and there, I knew we were going to have an amazing concert. I called Stan outside, and we both helped Jim walk to the stage where we placed his hands over the microphone that stood centerstage. As the curtain rose to the thunderous screams of adoring fans, the announcer barked, *"Ladies and gentlemen . . . THE DOORS!"*

Meanwhile, my relationship with Clapton continued with

his every visit to New York. I watched Cream perform a few songs at the annual "Murray the K" show and was totally destroyed by their musical mastery. I was invited to some of their recording sessions at Atlantic Records' studios for the upcoming album *Disraeli Gears*. And that's when the idea hit me!

The following day, I ran into the college newspaper office and waited for Stan to arrive. I had the next concert planned. *Fresh Cream* was already getting tons of FM radioplay, and the band's new release—a lot less bluesy—was certain, in my opinion anyway, to be an immediate hit. I begged Stan to book Cream for the Hunter concert series, and, after speaking with Delsener, they booked the band for two performance over a Friday and Saturday weekend, for about $2500.

The college auditorium was rockin' as a sold-out audience shouted its approval of every song from this virtuoso trio. I felt great. I managed to parlay my instinctive knowledge of what bands would be big, with my ability to verbally sell the idea to promoters. And although I was on a high this night, a "high" of another kind soon put a damper on my college days.

As music became more and more vital in my life, my thirst for an education diminished. Drugs only enhanced my appreciation for music and increased my lethargic attitude toward everything else. My mother always told me to finish college so I'd have a career to fall back on. I didn't listen, and left college to pursue a career in the music business. Although I never regretted going out on my own, I do regret never having received a college diploma. It would have looked cool hanging next to my wall of gold and platinum records.

Diving In

It was now 1970, and the drug-use/hippie days were over. It was time for me to go out and get a real job. I still managed the band, and we were one of the most popular rock groups in all of Brooklyn—where a relatively healthy music scene had blossomed. After all, drugs and music went hand-in-hand back in the sixties.

I hadn't thought of it at the time, but my collection of interviews from the Hunter Envoy gave me quite a list of professional credentials. Now all I needed was for someone to give a damn! I must admit that not having to go to school really opened up my schedule. I had virtually nothing to do all day long. I continued to write songs for Dust with my writing partner Richie Wise. In those days, very few bands had demo tapes. We just learned the new songs, rehearsed them, and then performed them live. I don't remember anyone ever asking me for a press package in 1970. Naturally, this meant that if someone of importance wanted to get into the band, he'd have to see a live show.

During that summer, I received a telephone call that changed my life forever. A friend of mine named Fred Holman, who I worked with on the college paper, called to tell me he was leaving his job at Cash Box magazine to go on tour with his band, Frontier. Knowing that I was a writer and into music, he wanted to offer me an opportunity to interview for the job.

Cash Box was one of the top three music industry trade magazines in the country. An opportunity to work for them comes once in a lifetime. I was there!

By the time I started my job at Cash Box, I had already turned twenty-three. I was hired as the country music editor and also put in charge of the international section of the mag. This gave me insight into a new genre of music for me and made me aware of what was selling around the world. For me, a higher degree of learning was taking place. This was the real music industry, and I was part of it. I had finally made it inside.

The editor of Cash Box in 1970 was a man named Irv Lichtman, my mentor, and the man who singlehandedly taught me everything I know about editing, writing press releases, news headlines, and putting together a magazine—skills I still use today, some thirty years later. I don't know where I would have been without Irv's belief and support.

While at Cash Box, I learned how to interface with real record companies and their promotion and publicity departments. The more questions I asked, the more knowledge I gained. I got firsthand information about the inner workings of the labels (the best reason of all to try to intern at a record company). I learned how they scheduled album releases, got records into the stores and on the radio, set concert tours, and how they decided which single to release from an album.

I watched how the Cash Box chart department called the radio stations and record stores to determine the weekly chart positions for the Top 100 singles in the country. I watched, I asked, and I learned.

In 1971, I was promoted to the position of associate editor, which gave me even more clout and credibility. I now wrote news stories, artist and industry features, and cover headlines. I also put the entire magazine together with Irv every week. I loved it. I couldn't get enough. In my three years at the magazine, I don't think I missed a single day. I felt like I'd died and went to heaven. I couldn't believe they were letting me do all of this neat stuff and then also paid me for it on Fridays!

Note No. 1

I'm not writing this for my ego. There are lessons to be learned from all of this. If you really want to get a jump start in the industry, try getting an intern position at Billboard or HITS magazines or at almost any major or indie record company. You'd be surprised at the things you can learn in a six-month stint.

Right about this time, Dust, the rock group I managed and wrote songs for, signed a recording contract with a small label called Kama Sutra, whose president was Neil Bogart—the same Neil Bogart who later ran Casablanca Records.

So now, while working at the magazine for eight hours a day, I also needed to spend an additional eight hours at night in the recording studio overseeing and coproducing (along with the three other members of the band) Dust's first album.

Although I had never been in a professional recording studio before, I was anxious to add the credit of "record producer" to my resume, which now only boasted an "associate

Kerner in the Studio
May 7th, 1971—my very first time in a professional recording studio as a record producer, with a rock band called Dust. Shown in the photo, from left to right: bassist Kenny Aaronson (Joan Jett, Bob Dylan, Hall & Oates), drummer Marc Bell (Marky Ramone), and my coproducing and songwriting partner at that time, Richie Wise. That's yours truly over on the far right.

editor" listing. I always felt that the more I knew, the more valuable I would be in the industry. If I could do five jobs extremely well, that gave me five opportunities of employment. *Remember: there are lots of people who can do one thing very well, but few who can do many things very well.* I wanted to be one of them.

Once in the studio, I took full advantage of our engineer, Harry Yarmark, who had engineered a plethora of hit singles for the Lovin' Spoonful and the Four Seasons, among others. I riddled him with one question after another about studio technique. The problem was, we knew what we heard in our heads, we just didn't know how to make it happen in the studio.

Working on that LP gave me some 200 hours of professional studio time and a "produced by" credit on the album. All in all,

I was glad to get back to my editor's desk full-time. The band did some tour dates but nothing really materialized, so Richie and I began writing songs for the next album.

During this time, I was beginning to make a name for myself as a music journalist. I interviewed some of the top people in the industry, including Clive Davis, Black Sabbath, Stevie Wonder, and John Lennon (soon after he moved to New York—and yes, I even asked him about the "Paul is dead" fiasco).

I was never a great writer, but I knew how to communicate thoughts and feelings through the written word. And I always wanted to learn more. That's the key—I asked questions. Remember, there is no such thing as a stupid question, only stupid people who don't ask questions!

Note No. 2

Another opportunity for internships is at public relations firms, who are always in need of people to file and deliver features and press releases to the trades. Also, recording studios always need runners and studio help. This is an incredible way to learn firsthand about the recording process and a great place to learn about the biz from the inside. Check the classifieds section in every issue of Music Connection magazine for jobs and internships available.

In the music business, you sometimes have to make your own luck, and that often means putting it all on the line for something you believe in. Richie and I were disappointed with the way the first Dust album turned out and wanted to handle the production of the second album ourselves. After all, we wrote all of the songs, arranged them, and knew their intricacies better than anyone.

In order to get the approval of the band, we needed permission from Neil Bogart, as label president. Neil, ever the shrewd one, made us this deal: He'd let me and Richie produce the second album, but if he didn't like it, he was going to drop the band from his label. It took us all of one second to agree to his terms.

Here's a case where we forced something to happen to prove ourselves and bet the farm that we'd come through. Another 200 hours later, and Richie and I emerged with a credit we had sought for a long time—an album that read, "Produced by Kenny Kerner & Richie Wise." A real record, distributed nationally that credited us with the production. We talked the label into a fold-out cover and bought, for $500, a one-time use of a painting by Frank Frazetta ("The Three Vikings") for the album's cover. The album charted on Cash Box and Billboard, and thus began my career as a record producer.

Note No. 3

Know your strengths and weaknesses. Because my partner, Richie Wise, was always into turning knobs and contributing to the overall sonic feel of the record, I let him deal with the engineer exclusively. My strength was in the organizational and business efforts of the project, the song selection, the lyrics, the vocal performances, the final mixes, and the sequencing of the songs. What was important to me was that the combined efforts of the partnership worked and produced many gold and platinum records. Let that be a lesson to all regarding studio work. It's not who does what but rather what was done!

The success of Dust's second album, which we called *Hard Attack,* prompted Bogart to throw me and Richie other artists to produce. For us, it meant more production money and more credits. For me especially, it meant two jobs from which I was earning an income. I was now putting my eggs in two baskets!

Bogart let us produce an artist named Exuma, who he claimed sold tons of records in foreign countries. Exuma was formerly on Mercury Records and was known as the Obeah Man—whatever that is. We made a couple of adequate records with him, and then the real test came.

Bogart gave us a record by a group called Gunhill Road that was produced by Kenny Rogers. All along, Bogart felt the production was wrong and thought it should be rerecorded as a bit of a novelty/nostalgia song with a bounce to it. He asked me and Richie to produce it exactly as he explained.

The Gunhill Road single, "Back When My Hair Was Short," peaked at #21 on the national charts and gave Richie and me our first real chart success. Our first Top 40 hit!

Note No. 4

Here's a case where Richie and I had to put our feelings for the song on the backburner and give the label president, the man paying all of the bills, exactly what he wanted—despite our production vision. A lesson in playing politics. I hope you guys reading this book are learning something from all of these experiences!

And while we're on the subject of politics, here's a lesson I learned the hard way—by being put between a rock and a hard place. The next project we worked on for Neil yielded us our only #1 single of our production career, but I never would have imagined it from the way the project took shape.

We were given a copy of a record called "Brother Louie" as recorded by a British band, Hot Chocolate, on a British label, RAK Records, that was owned by Mickie Most, a successful record producer. For some bizarre reason, Bogart heard this tale of interracial dating (black girl, white boy) as a hit for Exuma and wanted Richie and me to rerecord the song. As usual, we called our musician friends in a band called Stories to lay down the tracks for Exuma, and the plan was to have him do the vocals when the tracks were done. Nothing out of the ordinary. Because Stories was a real band, they played well together, and the tracks would be tight and on the money. So far, so good.

At this time in their career, Stories' manager was negotiating to pull the group off of Bogart's label, but we were not involved in those dealings. We just wanted the band members to cut a track, be paid for it, and do whatever their manager asked. This was *not* the first time we had hired the members of Stories to cut tracks for us.

Recording went great, and we ended up with a powerful track. But, because Exuma had never recorded or sung anything but his own material, we felt it was important to give him some kind of vocal guidelines to follow. So, we asked Stories' lead singer Ian Lloyd to go in and lay down a reference vocal for Exuma to follow. And that's when the problems began.

Lloyd went into the studio and delivered the first line of the song: "She was black, as the night, Louie was whiter than white . . ." and at the very same instant, both Richie and I looked at each other. Instinctively, we knew this was a hit record in the making—but for Stories, *not* Exuma.

Note No. 5

See the problems, now? 1) We were being paid to produce a single for Exuma. 2) If we finished the track with Stories, we'd encounter the wrath of their manager who wanted them off the label and did not want to give that label more material to release. 3) We had no authority to make a Stories record even though we thought it would be a hit! What to do? Are you beginning to see how simple situations can become tremendously political? Good.

What we did was both simple and logical. Since we were recording under the scenario of doing a complete reference vocal for Exuma to follow, we finished the Ian Lloyd vocals for the entire song and made a cassette copy of it. This meant that even if someone sabotaged the masters and erased Lloyd's vocal, we had a cassette of it to play for Bogart.

The next day, we played it for the president, and he went nuts. He ordered us to finish the entire song that same week so he could release it before the weekend. Mickie Most had already set in motion plans to release the Hot Chocolate, full-length version, through Columbia, here in America. We had no time to waste.

The very next night we were back in the studio doing master vocals with Ian when the band's manager arrived and ordered us to stop recording the song. We politely explained to him that we were instructed to complete the song for the new Stories single, and he hit the ceiling.

Richie and I had to decide, politically, where our loyalties were: Did they side with the band's manager, whose only interest was Stories, or did they side with Neil Bogart, who had been giving us work every day for months and respected our talents as producers? Duh! This was a no-brainer.

From start to finish, the Stories' version of "Brother Louie" was recorded, mixed, and released within a week. Mickie Most, releasing the original European version by Hot Chocolate through the Columbia/Epic distribution network, threatened to bury our version—counting on the money Columbia would put behind the record. Hot Chocolate picked up three radio stations, and the Stories version of "Brother Louie" not only hit #1, but stayed there for two weeks, becoming one of the biggest records of the year.

Note No. 6

"Going pro" also means being able to deal with situations in a professional manner. True, we could have blown off Exuma and Stories' manager, but by telling them that we were hired and paid by Neil Bogart and that we had to do what he wanted, we took ourselves right out of the picture. Now, if they had a problem, it was between them and Neil. We acted logically, rationally, and professionally!

Richie and I continued producing together, giving Bogart and his two labels (Buddah/Kama Sutra and Casablanca) many hits. We had a manager who, for a 30% commission, was supposed to get us work and take advantage of our current chart successes—but he sorta failed to parlay our hits into any kind of substantial production deal.

After a couple of years as a producer, I got tired of spending long, dark nights in a secluded recording studio waiting for a strange guitarist to play a meaningful solo. I was always fascinated by the totally creative areas of the business, and sitting still and powerless in a studio just didn't cut it for me anymore—despite the money and success.

I had this incredible idea. Studying the Billboard charts week after week, I noticed the popularity of several teen stars—Shaun Cassidy and Leif Garrett in particular. Though their talents were marginal, the combination of the right look and image, the right song, and the right marketing campaign made them successful chart-topping idols.

Here was my thinking: If these solo teen stars rose to incredible acceptance and success, it followed logically (to me, anyway) that an entire teen rock band of incredible-looking guys couldn't miss!

Note No. 7

Again, following through with the philosophy of "not putting all of your eggs in one basket," I continued to produce and earn a living while starting to develop a brand-new idea.

I called some of the people I knew in the music business and told them about my idea of putting together a teen rock band—an American Menudo, if you will. Those who didn't laugh, agreed to help me find the members. In my search, which lasted a year and a half, I went for image over talent. I figured that we could always rehearse rigorously and develop someone's talents, but I couldn't make anyone look great, even with all the rehearsing in the world.

When you live in Hollywood, telling people that you're looking for young, good-looking boys can get you into a lot of trouble. And maybe that's why it took me so long to come up with the five guys who finally made it into the band I named Virgin. You see, I wanted a name that meant different things to different people. I wanted a little sex and controversy thrown into the mix for good measure.

The guys in the band ranged in age from 14 to 17, and each could play an instrument with some degree of proficiency. There was no doubt that these guys would get incredible press in the teen magazines if only I could make something happen on a national level. But what?

We began rehearsing and listening to their original material. I picked the best of their songs and mixed in some covers to round out a set. We did an initial photo session that I serviced to the teen magazines just to get a reaction. And it worked. The editors called me back and said they were perfect—if only something real would happen.

I began to think, "Who did I know that might be interested in a young, teen band with an incredible image that could be marketed internationally?" And then it came to me: Bill Aucoin. The man who managed Kiss. Image. Music. Controversy. Marketing. All rolled up into one, neat package. I called Bill and told him about Virgin. He loved the name and promised to hook up with me to see one of their rehearsals on his next trip to the West Coast.

At this time in his career, Aucoin was on top of the management mountain. He was considered to be the god of personal managers—and wealthy beyond belief.

Note No. 8

My thinking was that if I could get Bill Aucoin to co-manage the band with me, I'd have a powerful manager on my side, and that would mean doors would fly open everywhere. It would also give the band professional credibility and present Aucoin with another creative challenge—which he loved.

I rehearsed the band three times a week, concentrating on the same six songs I wanted them to play for Bill. I also worked in some choreography to make it more interesting. Finally, the day of reckoning arrived.

We set the rehearsal for Studio F at S.I.R. Rehearsal Studios in Hollywood. Studio F was the smallest room available, but it made things pretty cozy. Bill came in all aglow, looking like a million bucks. We hugged, kissed, spoke for a bit, and then I introduced him to the individual members of the band. By the look on his face, I knew I had a better-than-average chance of pulling this off if only the band didn't blow it during their performance. The guys in Virgin all knew who Bill was, and believe me, they wanted it as much or more than I did.

It didn't take long for me to get my answer. The guys took the stage, the drummer counted off the first song, and after a second tune, Bill stopped the show, walked over to the band, and said, "I want to manage you." It was over. I did it.

We all congratulated each other and went home with our heads in the clouds thinking about the possibilities. For the band, it was a shot at stardom. For me, already a successful record producer, it was a shot at becoming a successful personal manager, too. We all slept pretty good that night.

Note No. 9

The lesson here is that it's great to come up with original ideas that seem to be out in left field somewhere, but you also need to research them to make certain they are valid. More importantly, if you really believe in the idea, stay with it. It took me almost two years just to find the right band members. I could easily have given up long before the mission was complete—but I believed that I had the right instincts and a good, sound idea worth pursuing.

I spent the next couple of days meeting with Bill to go over my game plan for the band and allowing him to meet with the guys alone. That's the part he liked best.

Bill went back to New York, and I continued to work with the band. Bill turned the day-to-day management chores over to his West Coast rep, Alan Miller, who ran Aucoin's Los Angeles offices. Miller went out and got the guys outfits to wear—colored French T-shirts with our Virgin logo on it and tight, white jeans. They were delirious. More importantly, however, it made them look and feel like a real band!

Several weeks later, Bill returned to Los Angeles and brought a guest down to the Virgin rehearsals—record producer Michael Lloyd, who, coincidentally, was looking for an act to open the national Shaun Cassidy tours. Again, after just a couple of tunes performed in their new band outfits, Virgin was named opening act on the upcoming Shaun Cassidy tour—forty-four cities in all.

What this meant was that the very first gig these guys got to play professionally was in front of 18,000 people in Salt Lake City, Utah. For me, it meant I could really go full-tilt with the teen press, now that their visibility was increased and they had the credibility of association with a real teen superstar. What followed was a period of about a year where Virgin was in every single teen magazine in the world. Sixteen magazine ran an unprecedented five-page, full-color, pull-out poster section on the band. Mail was delivered to the offices in huge canvas bags. On tour, the band needed bodyguards to keep the fans away. We preboarded airplanes to eliminate possible riots.

I traveled with the band as the legal guardian of the fifteen-year-old guitarist and got a mouthful of road dust. I loved every minute of it, yet I knew it was all for nothing. You see, although Virgin was clearly one of the most photographed bands in the world and one of the most popular teen bands in the country, we still were touring without having any product (record or poster) to sell.

Note No. 10

Touring for the experience is cool, if it's a club tour. But to tour arenas holding 15,000-20,000 people a night and to not have a record out to sell—even an indie record—is a real sin. When the Cassidy tour ended and the smoke cleared, Shaun had sold millions of singles and albums, and Virgin faded into oblivion because they left nothing behind with their fans, except memories. Given the same situation a second time, we'd still jump at it, because the experience and exposure alone was priceless. But as a career move, we gained little.

Lesson: Always weigh the advantages and disadvantages of a situation, and try to determine how it helps your career. Going on the Shaun Cassidy tour was a lot of fun, but not having a record or poster to earn revenue kept the band from moving to the next career level. A record could have been reviewed in the trades, could have received airplay, and maybe could have charted. A color poster would have earned us thousands of dollars. Unfortunately, at that time, we weren't able to pull off either.

Soon after the Virgin period, Aucoin's West Coast offices closed, and I took a job with a Los Angeles-based public relations firm. I wasn't really into PR, but I wanted to learn about how to get reviews and interviews and above all, to make some connections with the press that might help me at a later date.

My heart wasn't into the gig at all, but I held on for over three years and brought home a decent paycheck. Our company represented Jay Leno, Michael J. Fox, Body By Jake, and a few top models. I learned how to pitch stories to magazines and how to book tour press for artists. Again, it was another invaluable learning experience for me—making me even more well-rounded and knowledgeable than before. Now, I could add "public relations" to my growing professional arsenal that already included "record producer" and "personal manager." Each additional area of expertise I added made me more valuable to the music community.

When business really started to drag at the PR company, I was let go for financial reasons. And although I was pleased, it left me without a job. I was now more determined than ever to get back into the music side of things so I kept sending letters and resumes to various local music magazines and newspapers trying to get something going—anything.

Note No. 11

This is one of those times where persistence pays off. Forget about all of the people who slam doors in your face, and keep trying to find that one *door that will open so you can walk through.*

After a few months of "pounding the pavement," as they say, I received a call from Bud Scoppa who, at that time in his career, was the senior editor of Music Connection magazine, a Los Angeles-based music mag with a focus on the local scene. Bud asked me over to the office (he had already received several calls and a resume) and gave me the chance of a lifetime. He had a cover story in the works called "Rock Grows Up," and he wanted me to edit it and rework some of it. Somehow, I had to turn this opportunity into a full-time paying job.

I took the story home and began reading it when another idea hit me. If I could somehow show Bud that I was aggressive and not afraid of hard work, maybe he'd call me more often for rewrites. I called him on the phone and told him that rather than rewrite a weak story, I'd like to write a brand new one from scratch. Incredulous as it seemed to him, I was willing to take on an awful lot of work with a deadline staring me in the face. Scoppa agreed and told me to bring the story back to his office at 8:30 a.m. the following morning. That didn't leave me much time at all.

I drove home and upon arriving, put the story away for the time being. I set my alarm clock to wake me at about 4:00 a.m. and went about my daily business.

I awoke early the next morning and after putting up a pot of hot coffee, jumped right into the story, completing it by 7:45. Plenty of time to spare. I showered and drove to meet Bud, getting there fifteen minutes earlier than expected. To make a long story short, that was my first feature ever in Music Connection magazine. A short while later, Scoppa and publisher Michael Dolan hired me as the magazine's associate editor. I spent about two years as associate editor before replacing Scoppa as senior editor for some eight years—longer than any other senior editor in the magazine's history.

Note No. 12

Though my job at MC was one of the most rewarding I've ever had in the industry, I used it to build connections with the entire A&R community when I reformatted the magazine's A&R Report column to an interview-only format. This gave me the opportunity to speak with a different A&R person every issue and cultivate a relationship with them—one I still have today! I was now able to tie my A&R and record company contacts to my experience as a personal manager. This gave me more clout in the business. Contacts = clout!

These days, I still write for several national music magazines (Gig, Music Biz, Music Paper), teach full-time at Musicians Institute, manage a band (Cartoon Boyfriend) that is currently the most popular, best-drawing band in Los Angeles and well on its way to international success, and I just finished up this book. Don't wait for the sequel, guys.

The year 2000 will mark my thirtieth year in the music business. Have I made the millions I dreamed of? No. Am I pissed? No. How many people get to really enjoy their jobs in life? How many look forward to going to work each day? How many truly love teaching others how to do things right?

If you're now setting sail for a career in the music business, realize that your chances of success are few. If you're aspiring to become the new guitar god, also think about what you can do with that guitar if you don't quite make it to god-status—like guitar lessons, session player, etc.

The two predominant philosophies in this business are: 1) to put all your eggs in one basket, focus, and go for broke, or 2) to keep learning and experiencing and be good at many things so you have longevity and many successes. Fifty dollars at the blackjack tables in Vegas will allow you to play for hours. Bet a thousand on 19-red and lose, and you're finished!

"Going pro" is both an attitude and a lifestyle. It's a means by which you can gain self-confidence by knowing how to interface with those who might intimidate you or otherwise be inaccessible. It is a mentality that tells you to keep educating yourself. Keep reading the trades. Keep asking questions. Again, in this business, it's not how many times you get knocked down but how many times you get back up. It's all about how you keep on keepin' on!

I love dreamers. I dreamed with Kiss and was successful beyond my wildest imagination. (I helped them get signed to Casablanca records and coproduced their first two albums, both of which went platinum—a story for another time.) I dreamed as a producer and achieved far beyond my grasp. As a publicist, an editor, a journalist, a teacher, and a manager, I reached places that transcended dreams. But always, I dreamed with my head in the clouds and one foot firmly planted on the ground.

The End.

No Way!

Review: Q&A

Though the music business as we know it has no rules, there is a certain knowledge you must possess to be able to play the game effectively; while the industry's "no rules" doctrine really gives every player a fair chance at the pot of gold at the end of the platinum rainbow, it also allows for some very complicated roadblocks!

This chapter is intended to provide you with the ammunition needed to get started in the music business. It answers some of the most frequently asked questions covering almost every area of the biz—from bands to managers to touring to publishing and then some. Much of this material is discussed elsewhere in the book, but I'm also presenting it in this format as both a quick review and an easy reference guide. It's written in simple Q&A form: first you read the question and then the answer. In some cases, where there is a rather complicated query, a recommendation might be made to check out another source of industry information for more details. These instances are rare.

For years, I taught classes in Music Business Education at UCLA and Musicians Institute, and I was always amazed at the amount of misinformation that ran rampant within this industry. Everyone has an opinion, it seems. Yet, in most instances, there is clearly a right way and a wrong way of doing things. The information presented in this text gives you the right way of handling your career in the music business.

The questions in this book were selected because they were asked repeatedly over my thirty-year career in this industry. In each case, I have attempted to answer them simply and directly so that they can be understood by everyone—from the fledgling artist to the wiley veteran. My years as a record producer, songwriter, personal manager, journalist, publicist, and teacher have allowed me to experience the music industry to its fullest. You are now the beneficiaries of that experience. Drink deep... and go pro!

How do I legally copyright a song?

According to United States copyright law, you have a copyright as soon as you can make a "tangible" copy of something. Because the word "tangible" really means something that you can touch, in the music business, that translates to writing a song down on paper and then making a tape copy of it on a cheap cassette recorder. Legally, that's a copyright.

Do I have to register my song with the U.S. Copyright Office in Washington, D.C. to have a copyright?

No. Although by doing so you get some exclusive rights—such as the right to reproduce your work, to manufacture your work, to make a derivative copy of your work, to display your work, and to distribute your work.

How long does a copyright last?

The length of a copyright for a work created after January 1st, 1978 is the duration of the life of the author plus seventy years—or, *life plus seventy,* as we call it. Again, you can call or write to the copyright office and obtain, free of charge, Form PA, for the copyright of a musical composition containing music and lyrics or just music.

Do I mail myself a package with my tapes in it ("poor man's copyright") and not open the package?

No. You do not get any exclusive rights with this method, nor do you have any more of a copyright than if you simply wrote the song down and made a tape of it.

Realistically, it does make sense to fill out a Form PA from the U.S. Copyright Office because—in addition to the exclusive rights this gives you—they actually stamp a date on your return certificate which puts a time frame on your creation.

Can more than one person own the same song and copyright?

Yes. When you sit down and write a song with your friend or band mate, you have a "joint work" or a "joint copyright." If both of you wrote the song equally—meaning you both contributed to the words and the music—then you can each receive 50% ownership of that song and copyright. The actual percentages are predetermined by the writers based on each one's contribution to the finished song. Remember that each of you owns part of the words and part of the music, regardless of what part of the actual song you wrote!

If someone in my band writes a song with me and then leaves the band, who can use that song?

Once you own a song as a writer, you own that song unless you are foolish enough to sell your writer's share. The fact that you are no longer in the same band as the other writer has absolutely nothing to do with ownership. In fact, here's a very interesting scenario: Suppose that Sean and Bobby are songwriters in the same band, and in 1995 they cowrite a song called "Love Wins Again." Several months later, citing irreconcilable differences, Sean leaves the band and decides to put his song "Love Wins Again" in a movie soundtrack while Bobby, furious over the decision, wants to save that same song for inclusion on his first record album. What happens? Does "Love Wins Again" wind up in a movie soundtrack or on Bobby's album?

The answer is really a lot simpler than this scenario. Since *both* writers own the same song, each can do with it as he pleases. Therefore, "Love Wins Again" will be recorded on an album and will also appear on a soundtrack—and in each case, both Sean *and* Bobby will be credited as the writers.

If I write all of the songs for my band, should I split the publishing income with the other members?

This is a tough one, and the answer is, really, to do whatever you think is in the best interest of the band. The concept of a single band writer sharing his publishing royalties (*not* the writer's royalties) with band mates who did not write, was an attempt to give everyone extra money so that the writer didn't wind up living in a mansion on the hill and the rest of the band in a cardboard box under the freeway! Giving someone money for nothing is not something I personally believe in, but it does help keep bands together longer. And why not? Who can turn down money for not working!

Since the real issue here is to make every band member feel he is an equal member, it seems justifiable to give everyone just a "taste" of the publishing royalties—say 10% each—while the sole songwriter keeps the remaining percentages for himself. Remember, the publishing royalties on a platinum album are nothing to sneeze at.

How do I protect the name of my band?

Simple. By using it! The best way to be sure nobody else comes up with the same name as your band is to keep it in the public's eye. When you play a show, be certain your band is listed in the newspaper calendar sections. When you make band photos, include the band's name at the bottom of the picture for identification purposes. Also, try to get local magazines and newspapers to write small press items about your band.

Save all of these things in a separate file, and make sure they are dated. Should you discover another band is using your name, you will be able to prove that you had it first and that you are showing good faith by keeping the band's name active. This method is far less expensive and less complicated than writing to the Secretary of State's office and getting a service mark for your band. But, should you decide to go the "official" route, you will still need to present your file of clippings showing usage of your band's name.

What is a "performing rights organization"?

ASCAP, BMI, and SESAC, all known as performing rights organizations, are charged with the responsibilities (among others) of issuing checks to affiliated publishers and writers for the performances and licensing of their songs. Just as record companies pay mechanical royalties based on records sold, PROs pay performance royalties based on radio and TV play, live performances, jukebox play, etc. As a publisher, you may affiliate a publishing company with all three PROs, but a writer has to choose only one.

What items should my press kit contain?

Press kits (or press packages as they are also called), should contain your photo (a recent one), a brief bio, one or two press clippings and a demo tape with *no more than three* of your best songs. Be certain there is a contact name and phone number prominently displayed within your package. Do not stuff your package with a complete history of the world, as nobody will take the time to read it. You want to focus on the music and not the history of the band or artist.

What tips can you give me regarding my demo tape?

First of all, remember that demo stands for "demonstration." This should not be a master-quality tape that costs you thousands of dollars and takes a year to record. Make sure that your tape sounds as professional as possible within a reasonable amount of time.

Also, be certain that you record your *best* songs and not necessarily the songs your friends like best. There is a big difference. The songs should be focused and should sound like the same band is playing the same kind of music throughout the entire tape. Don't confuse matters by showing off your versatility and recording a country song, a punk anthem, a ballad, and a dance track. By doing that, you will only confuse those trying to determine what it is you really do and how to sell your music to an audience.

Limit your demo to a maximum of three songs or a total of

about 12-15 minutes. Nobody has all day to spend listening to your tape. Include a lyric sheet so people can follow along and hear what you are singing.

If your tape has to be rewound before it is played, expect it to be trashed immediately. The object is to make it as easy and enjoyable as possible for someone to hear your music. Rewinding your tape at the onset does not fall into that category.

Most important is to make sure the tape really does sound like the band. There is nothing more frustrating than for someone to fall in love with your tape only to be totally disappointed when he hears you play live. There's got to be a consistency. Make it so.

What is an "unsolicited" tape?

An unsolicited tape is simply a demo tape that was not called for by someone in an A&R capacity. If you decide to be aggressive and mail your band's demo tape to the Capitol Records A&R department, that tape is considered "unsolicited" and will most likely be either returned to you unopened or thrown in the trash. A&R reps do this because they receive thousands of tapes and want to limit the number of submissions to only those that they themselves ask for. Also, they don't want to be held legally responsible if, two years down the road, you hear a song on the radio that sounds suspiciously like the one you sent in to an A&R rep. Any tape sent in by a manager, attorney, agent, promoter, journalist, etc. is usually accepted and considered to be solicited!

Should an attorney shop my demo tape?

There is no right answer to this question. My belief is that since attorneys spend most of their schooling studying music business *law,* they should stick to law. After all, if you wanted to get your shoes shined, you wouldn't bring them to a bakery! Most attorneys are good at law—paperwork, contracts, litigation, negotiations, letter writing. So what makes them music mavens? What makes them able to tell a great song from a mediocre one?

One of the most prevalent scams in the music business today is attorney demo-shopping. Here's how it works. A lawyer will ask you to give him about ten to fifteen copies of your demo tape and, for a fee (usually ranging from $500-$2500 plus expenses), he will get your tapes to the right people at the right labels. Sounds like a great deal—until you discover that he is providing this same service to a dozen other bands at the same time! And many packages that get sent out contain three to four tapes so the attorney can save on costs for postage and supplies while charging you as if it went out under separate cover!

Now riddle me this: How can an attorney effectively shop a dozen acts at the same time? He can't. But people fall into this trap because it sounds enticing, and they are desperate. Desperate people do desperate things. If you absolutely must allow a music attorney to shop your tapes, ask him to provide the following: a list of who he is sending the tapes to, a guarantee that your tape will go out alone, and a written follow-up with comments from every A&R person who listened to the tape. Chances are this will be too much work for the attorney.

Keep in mind that since most attorneys will be working on a retainer fee (you pay them in advance for a certain amount of work), their interest is in prolonging this arrangement and thereby increasing their income. If you can find a relatively new, hungry attorney who is aggressive and believes in your music, then this shopping somehow makes sense. Otherwise, it's much ado about nothing.

Most of the top-level, high-powered attorneys will not shop tapes but will represent unsigned bands for a fee, usually 5% of the artist's gross income. If this is the case, you have nothing to lose. For that percentage, the attorney does all of your paperwork and isn't paid a cent until you earn money. But he first has to truly believe that you will be a major success.

How many songs should I put on my demo tape?

The real purpose of your demo tape is to show industry movers and shakers that you (or your band) can write great songs and perform them well. You want these decision makers to listen to all of the music you've sent them. Therefore, you cannot take up half of their day with your tape! My recommendation is to put no more than three of your best songs on any demo tape—and be sure it does not exceed fifteen minutes of playing time.

This will give everyone a short overview of your capabilities and reason to ask for more music if there is genuine interest. Also, before you mail tapes out, check to see that there is a current contact name and telephone number on each and every tape. Record companies can't call you if they don't have your number!

What are "dummy lyrics"?

Dummy lyrics are words you scribble down on paper to help you remember how to sing a melody. Paul McCartney offers the best example of this. Before completing the finished version of his classic song "Yesterday," McCartney wanted to be sure he remembered the melody of the song until he got around to writing the final words. So, in place of the final title, he sang the words "Scrambled Eggs." You'll note that "scrambled eggs" and "yesterday" both have three syllables when sung. Yes-ter-day and scram-bled eggs. Get it? Once he sat down to finally complete the song, he tossed out the "scrambled eggs" and put the word "yesterday" in its place. This is a classic example of using dummy lyrics.

Should I move to Los Angeles, New York, or Nashville to get a record deal?

Not necessarily. Most A&R executives have a budget that includes money for traveling around the country to find new talent. If you are a "big fish in a small pond," so to speak, you will stand out even more in your hometown. Coming to Los Angeles, New York, or Nashville will only complicate things for you. There are far too many acts in those cities already, and you will become "just another band."

Stay where you are. Become the biggest band in your area. Someone there (a club booking agent, a local journalist, a record store owner, a radio station personality) will discover you and try to get in touch with someone at a record company. Contrary to what you believe, most bands are discovered in their local areas and not in the City of Angels, the Big Apple, or the home of the Grand Ole Opry. However, if you are a hot country artist, moving to Nashville would make things easier. Everyone else stay put!

What are the responsibilities of a personal manager?

There are no limits to the responsibilities of a personal manager. In addition to being the visionary for the artist—the person charged with guiding, directing, and fulfilling an artist's career in the music business—the personal manager must also be a good listener, a problem solver, a babysitter, psychologist, psychiatrist, social worker, negotiator, friend, confidant, business partner, and just about everything else you can think of.

A good personal manager must understand the needs and wants of the *person* as well as the artist. He must know that unless the *person* is focused, the artist within will never be able to make a run at success.

Who can become a personal manager in the music industry?

Anyone who wants to. Unlike most other jobs within the same industry, personal managers are not certified and need no license or education to operate. Pretty scary, huh? They simply call themselves "personal managers" and go about the business of ruining careers! Because there are no prerequisites for becoming a manager, the selection of a reputable PM is made all the more difficult. So ask a lot of questions, and choose carefully.

How much should I pay my personal manager?

Almost all personal managers work on a commission basis; they receive a percentage of the artist's gross income. That means that the manager is paid before an artist can deduct a single cent from his income. Most managers get somewhere between 10% and 20% of the gross. The actual percentage they receive depends on how "heavy" the manager is, what his responsibilities will be, and what the artist is willing to pay him. Also, the more powerful the artist, the smaller the percentage typically received by the manager. There's nothing wrong with getting 5% of Bruce Springsteen's gross income!

On rare occasions, a personal manager will ask to receive a commission of 25% but will pay the artist's booking agency fee from his commissions. If that's the case, put it in writing in the management contract before you sign.

Can a personal manager commission all of an artist's income?

Yes. However, the key word here is "income." When a record company gives an artist $150,000 specifically for paying a record producer and recording an album, that money is *not* income. When that same label contributes $75,000 to help that band stay on its tour (tour support), that money isn't considered income, either. In most cases, money given to an act to record, to pay a record producer, and to stay on tour, is not commissioned by personal managers. But again, you must put this in writing before you sign with your manager.

How do I limit how much money my manager gets after his contract expires and he no longer represents me?

As an artist, you have to understand two basic things. First, that you probably will be around long after your manager's contract expires. Second, that the time to take care of these things is at the very beginning of your relationship with a manager and not when you're worth millions and you're trying to ace him out!

Here's a very common manager-artist scenario: You sign a five-year management contract, and, after four years have expired, your manager is successful in getting you a recording contract. Label negotiations take two months, rehearsals and preproduction take two months, and the recording and mastering of the album take three months. By the time your record is officially released, your manager's contract has expired.

As fate would have it, you sign on with a new, giant management firm, and coincidentally, almost a year later, your album explodes and sells five million copies. Your first manager, the man who hasn't worked for your career in a year, is legally entitled to his total commissions on that monstrous album, and you also have to pay full commissions to your new management company. What this means is that you might be in a position where it could cost you 40% in management fees!

To remedy this situation, there exists something called the "sunset clause," which limits the amounts of money paid to a personal manager after his contract expires. How does it work? Simple—you make it up! You and your manager sit down before signing and come up with an agreement that is *mutually acceptable* to both parties.

One possibility is to decide that for all deals entered into during the term of the management contract, your manager will receive full commissions, but on product released after the termination or expiration of the management contract, he will receive half commissions for the first year, then a third of the commissions, then a quarter, and then nothing. This gives your former manager additional income for his efforts and still cuts him off from collecting funds forever.

The key here is to take care of this before you sign the contract. After the ink dries, your manager will be very reluctant to give back monies that he feels is rightfully due him. And always remember to negotiate in good faith. Your final resolution must satisfy both parties.

What are the functions of a business manager, and how do they differ from those of a personal manager?

When an artist reaches the point in his career when loads of royalties are pouring in, and he is forever on the road touring, he will need to hire a business manager to help pay his bills and take care of his finances while he's traveling. The BM might send him a prearranged weekly allowance, pay his rent/mortgage, invest his money, and get those child support checks out on time. A business manager has absolutely nothing to do with an artist's music or career. He works with money and numbers only. It is the artist's personal manager who is responsible for guiding and directing his career in the music industry.

How is a business manager paid?

Most business managers get a percentage of the artist's gross income—usually in the area of 5%. Many times, they will work on an hourly basis or on a pre-approved monthly fee. Remember, though, that if you're not making lots of money, you will *not* need the services of a business manager. In many cases, your local accountant will provide similar services for much less of a fee.

How is a booking agent paid?

Like personal managers, booking agents are paid a percentage of the artist's gross—usually 10%—and usually only on a tour that the agent books for that artist. In other words, if an agent books a tour guaranteeing the act $10,000 per show, that agent will automatically deduct his $1,000 commission from each paycheck. He is not entitled to commission record royalties or merchandising or publishing—only monies derived from personal appearances.

Unlike a personal manager, an agent must be licensed by the state to legally provide his services. On the other hand, a personal manager may not (especially in the state of California) act as an agent in obtaining employment for his artists. This stipulation is made clear in all personal management contracts. A personal manager may work out the specifics of a tour or an isolated show with the agent, but he cannot procure the employment. Many times, agents will require the artist to sign a contract for a term of a year so that no other agents can book the act.

How is it possible for a musician/band to make tons of money yet have so little left over for himself? Where does all this money go?

This is a question I've been asked over and over again. But if you've been paying attention, the answer shouldn't come as a surprise. The best way I can explain it is to give you a real example of monies earned and monies paid out in commissions. See if you can follow this.

A band at the professional level will almost always have assembled its pro team which consists of a personal manager, a business manager, an attorney, and a booking agent. Here are the commissions each typically takes:

Manager	20% of the gross income
Business manager	5% of the gross income
Attorney	5% of the gross income
Booking agent	10% of performance monies

Let us assume that there is a four-piece rock band that is getting $10,000 per live performance. Immediately, upon receipt of that money, a cool 40% is deducted to pay the band's pro-team members. The manager receives $2,000, the business manager takes away $500, the attorney gets $500, and the agent gets $1,000. So, with $4,000 deducted immediately, the band is left with $6,000. But we're not done yet!

We must now deduct another 10% for the additional salaries of tour managers, road managers, and drivers, as well as for miscellaneous show expenses. That leaves $5,000 left for the band to split amongst four players. Dividing that equally means that each member of the band receives $1,250 of the $10,000 gross. After taxes, an individual member is lucky to be left with about $1,000 for himself.

Where did all the money go, you asked? Where, indeed!

What does a publisher do, and how are they paid?

A writer assigns his song copyrights to a publishing company, and in exchange, a publisher promises the songwriter to get others to record his songs, to license his songs, to make sure the writer gets paid, to handle all of the paperwork/business involved in these transactions, and to split the money with the writer. These activities—finding others to record songs, issuing licenses, paying the writer, and collecting money—are called "administration rights."

In most cases, the publisher and the writer split all income 50/50. The publisher generally uses his 50% to cover his expenses and profit—this is called the publisher's share—while the remaining 50% is called the writer's share. The publisher exercises extreme power in that only he can decide who can record a song for the very first time.

The publisher will issue licenses to record companies, allowing them to use songs on records in exchange for that record company paying the publisher a designated amount (usually a few pennies) for all records manufactured and sold. Keep in mind that these pennies add up when your album—say, the soundtrack to *Forrest Gump,* for example, which has sold in excess of 5 million copies worldwide—goes multiplatinum. And I oughta know; I produced a song that was used on that soundtrack!

Writers and publishers are also paid each time their songs are performed on radio, on television, or in movies. These monies are collected by the performing rights organizations—ASCAP, BMI, and SESAC—and paid to the publishers who in turn pay writers their share of the income.

What is the Harry Fox Agency?

The Harry Fox Agency and its Canadian counterpart, the CMRRA (Canadian Mechanical Rights Reproduction Agency), issue mechanical licenses for publishers.

As you are aware, all record companies need to obtain licenses (permission) to record songs that are owned by publishing companies. Since it would take virtually all day long for each publisher to wallow through the miles of paperwork necessary to complete, mail, and verify these licenses, the Harry Fox Agency opened to work on these licenses exclusively.

These two agencies really act as an agent of the publishing companies in issuing the various licenses, making sure the users pay, and even auditing the record companies on occasion. For the services they provide, the Harry Fox Agency charges $4^1/_2$%—and the CMRRA, 5%—of the monies they collect.

How can I get an A&R job?

The quickest way to get a record company A&R job is to turn someone on to an act that they fall in love with and eventually sign. You can do this as a manager, agent, mailroom worker—you name it. The classic industry story is that of one-time A&R giant, Tom Zutaut, who convinced Elektra to sign Los Angeles rock band Mötley Crüe and was later hailed as a hero and given an A&R gig with Elektra. Zutaut has since become legendary in A&R lore. But what's he done lately? And where is he now?

Be persistent—find a band that you like and that will probably translate to record sales in other areas. Think about what record company needs this particular band. Don't recommend that a kiddie-label sign a great streetwise rap group. Be prepared to logically explain to an executive why you think this band should be signed. Have the facts ready. Be prepared to take the A&R exec to a local show or rehearsal at a moment's notice. And stick with your belief. You may have to bring several labels down to see this band before a single person gets it!

Today, most labels like new bands to release their own indie records and go through some of the same processes that the actual labels do—sales, promotion, marketing, touring, merchandising. This tells the record company that the act is familiar with the business of music and helps in the label's decision-making process. It also serves to give the band much-needed touring experience and helps build a very solid fan base in many different markets.

Other than signing new talent, what are the responsibilities of the A&R departments at record companies?

Oddly enough, the primary responsibility of A&R is to develop the careers of the artists that are already signed to the label. Most people picture A&R reps getting to their offices at about 11 in the morning, leaning back in their chairs and listening to tapes for five to six hours, making a few phone calls, and then hanging out at a local club until 4 a.m. Nothing could be further from the truth.

As an A&R person, you must be able to match record producers with your bands. You must be able to make a record album and oversee the studio goings-on of your acts. You have to deal with management and publishing and publicity. Most importantly, you must be able to convince the sales and promotion departments at your own label that your acts are the best and most important in the world. Not to mention doing recording budgets, traveling the country to see your acts while on the road, attending label conventions, doing demo and/or development deals, and, oh yes, keeping abreast of talent across the country so that you are first when it comes to signing that "next big thing."

For the record, A&R is one of the toughest gigs in the industry. Your job is always on the line. Sign one band that doesn't happen, and you've probably cost your boss half a million dollars. Do it twice, and you'll lose your job!

What is a "key man" clause?

Apart from a personal manager, a record company A&R person is the most vital cog in an artist's career in that he alone can sign that act to a recording contract. It is the A&R person who must discover the act, develop the act, sign the act, and then sell the virtues of that act to the remainder of his label executives so that they all work in unison toward the success of that act.

To insure that this A&R person remains in the artist's corner, many artists will attempt to include a clause in their recording contract which stipulates that this particular A&R person is a "key man" in the artist's career, and that should, for any reason, he no longer work at that label (he may be fired or leave for more money elsewhere), the artist, too, is free to leave the record company.

Lots of times, an A&R executive will force an act onto his label (because he has sole signing power) when nobody else on that label believes in the act. Then, just about the time the act's record is to be released, the exec jumps ship for a more lucrative job across town, leaving the poor act without a single friend or believer at the label and a debut album about to be shipped. What do you think the chances are of that album becoming successful?

If you're beginning to think that this "key man" clause is important, you're right! Tell your personal manager that you want that clause added to your recording contract when negotiations begin. It's worth fighting for under the right circumstances. However, most labels will not allow it to be part of the deal.

What is a "key member" clause?

If you ever took a look at the credits on an album, you'd notice that, in most cases, all of the songs were written by one or two of the members of the same group. Lennon and McCartney wrote most of the classics for the Beatles; Jagger and Richards, for the Rolling Stones; etc. In those bands, John Lennon, Paul McCartney, Mick Jagger, and Keith Richards would be considered "key members." If one or both of them left their respective bands, those bands would not be the same.

When signing a band today, A&R execs like to determine which of the members are the most vital to that band's creative process. After all, one of the major reasons for signing that band is because of those creative members. So, labels will sometimes include a "key member" clause in their recording contracts, stating that, in the event one of these members leaves (and these members must be clearly designated prior to signing), the label can decide if it wants to terminate the band's recording deal or continue with a replacement member.

Oftentimes, the band itself, at a meeting with their attorney to complete their partnership or corporation papers, will designate one or two members as key members.

One of the problems with the designation of key members is ego. It won't take long for the lead singer and lead guitarist (in a band, these are usually the members responsible for writing much of the material) to ask for more money, more points, or top billing. Their argument is simple: If I'm a key member, shouldn't I be paid more? My feeling is that all men are created equal. And if these key members do most of the writing, their reward is additional income via publishing and writing royalties and merchandising—not to mention all of the added publicity.

What are "all-in" royalties?

As compensation for records sold, recording artists are paid royalties, or "points," based on the volume of sales and the cost of the records. Additionally, the record producer is also paid in points. "All-in" royalties means that the artist himself is responsible for paying the producer's share of royalties. So, if an artist's deal calls for the band to receive royalties of fourteen points all-in, and the producer's fee is four points, this means the artist royalty is really ten points. Ten points for the band, plus four points for the producer, equals the fourteen points paid by the record company. Just think of it as "all-included."

Recommended Sources

Well, this is the final checklist you guys will have to look at—until my next book, that is. I just thought I'd put together a short list of music business-related books and magazines that you might find enjoyable and educational. Some are cool to use for reference, and others you might want to read from cover to cover. You decide. I've also included a few organizations that are worth checking out.

Books

All You Need to Know About the Music Business

by Donald S. Passman

If you really want an easy-to-read, easy-to-understand overview of the entire music industry, this is the book to buy—after you've bought mine, naturally. Passman is a high-powered music attorney with lots of important clients. His book, in addition to having a sense of humor, covers such important topics as merchandising, royalties, touring, publishing, sampling songs, motion picture music, and performer deals in addition to the necessary basics of management, copyrighting, attorneys, and agents. Buy this book.

The Craft and Business of Songwriting

by John Braheny

Braheny, in addition to being one of the good guys of the business, has written a book that is a must for all songwriters.

Tips on composition, lyrics, melodies—you name it—all with examples of current songs so you get his points. This makes for a great reference book that you'll turn to over and over again. I still use it today. Essential reading.

All Area Access: Personal Management for Unsigned Musicians
by Marc Davidson

Here's a very current book that looks at the important role of the personal manager and his relationship with unsigned local musicians. Deals with the day-to-day problems of trying to get an act signed and successful through the eyes and mind of the manager. Fascinating reading, and sheds light on the intricacies of management otherwise not known. Very realistic.

Successful Artist Management
by Xavier Frascogna, Jr. and H. Lee Hetherington

Since we've gone to press, the authors have changed the name of this book, but the info inside remains valuable for potential managers everywhere. This one looks at music business personal management from both perspectives—the artist and the manager. Chapters on establishing a relationship, planning a career, coping with success. Also includes sample contracts.

This Business of Music
by Sidney Shemel and M. William Krasilowsky

As the former TV character Sergeant Joe Friday used to say on Dragnet, "Just the facts, m'am." And that's exactly what you get with this voluminous text. Page after page of music business info written as a college text might read—no humor, just pages of copy. An important book to have, but certain topics are difficult for beginners. Leave this one at home for reference.

A&R Registry
published by The Music Business Registry, Inc.

Wanna get insider information on the A&R community, TV

and film supervisors, music attorneys, publishers, and publishing companies? Need accurate names, addresses, phone and fax numbers? This is the only place to go! Call 818-769-2722. These directories are for pros only. Published by music business veterans who really care.

Magazines

Music Connection

Published every other Thursday, this Los Angeles-based magazine covers the industry with an eye on L.A. You get a free directory in every single issue, so they're invaluable throughout the entire year. Comprehensive listings of managers, publishers, labels, producers, bands, attorneys, retail stores, music educators, video directors—and all with updated names, addresses, and telephone numbers. Yearly subscription is only about $40.

Billboard

They don't call this "The Bible of the Music Business" for nothing. Known the world over for its dozens of charts, Billboard also offers a plethora of additional music biz info on new labels, up-and-coming artists, record reviews, new signings, executives on the move, and their special issues on record manufacturers, Latin music, specialty labels, publishing, religious music, etc. This is expensive if you want a subscription, so you might want to buy one issue every two or three weeks just to keep abreast of the real deal.

Helpful Organizations

TAXI

No, this is not a car that takes you places, it is an independently-owned and operated A&R company that helps fledgling and veteran songwriters get their music out to other industry personnel. This membership-only company has some eighty-five tape screeners (all active participants in the music business) who critique each and every song that is submitted. The criticism is both about the writer's strong points as well as his/her weaknesses. Exceptional songs are forwarded on to record companies, publishers, music libraries, etc. TAXI does not take a commission on any deals that are made between a writer and other company. Membership fees: $299.95 per year, which also includes twelve monthly newsletters and free admission to the yearly Road Rally—an industry seminar with panels, discussions, and open mic night. Call: 818-888-2111.

Musicians Institute

For over twenty-five years, MI has been teaching the craft of performing on an instrument and playing live. But recently, they've added an extensive Music Business Education program to their curriculum. This program includes classes in A&R, publishing, personal management, songwriting, publicity and marketing, and a twenty-week overview of the music industry in general. Call: 213-860-1114.

PROs and the U.S. Copyright Office

For songwriters, membership in one of the three major performance rights organizations—ASCAP, BMI, and SESAC—is essential. Each organization has offices in major cities like New York, LA, Chicago, and Nashville and offers a wealth of services to its members—including workshops, showcases, grants and awards, and information and networking possibilities. For more info, contact them on the World Wide Web:

http://www.ascap.com/
http://www.bmi.com/
http://www.sesac.com/

For more information on copyrights, or to obtain a Form PA, try the following website:

http://lcweb..loc.gov/copyright/

About the Author

Kenny Kerner was living in New York City, writing for his college newspaper, and singing in a local band when, in 1970, a friend offered him a job at Cash Box magazine. His multi-faceted career in the music business has now spanned nearly three decades.

As a producer, he has garnered eighteen gold and platinum records for his work with Kiss, Gladys Knight & The Pips, Jose Feliciano, and Badfinger.

As a songwriter, he has co-written over three hundred songs, many of which have appeared in albums and on film.

As an editor and journalist, he has been a regular contributor to Music Connection, Metal Mania, Rock Scene, Music Biz, HITS, Gig, and Music Paper magazines—and interviewed such musical legends as Clive Davis, John Lennon, Stevie Wonder, Dick Clark, Steven Tyler, and Michael Jackson.

As a publicist, he has represented celebrities ranging from Jay Leno to Michael J. Fox to Body By Jake.

In addition to his current columns, which appear both in print and online, Kenny now teaches music business classes at Musicians Institute in Hollywood, California, and heads up Kerner Entertainment, a Los Angeles-based personal management company that specializes in finding and developing new talent.